TEACHING JOHN

Unlocking the Gospel of John for the Bible Teacher

DICK LUCAS & WILLIAM PHILIP

This book is short, unusual and valuable. Its aim is to help those who want to preach and teach from John's Gospel. However, it does not pretend to be a commentary. It will not replace exegetical work. Rather, it seeks to provide a key by which the expositor can extract the essential message of John's Gospel in his exposition. It is all the better for being a short work (and 'no more than a primer' in the authors' words, designed simply to 'whet the appetite'). It is a model of succinct clarity.

Robert Strivens
The Banner of Truth Magazine

TEACHING
JOHN

Unlocking the Gospel of John for the Bible Teacher

DICK LUCAS & WILLIAM PHILIP

SERIES EDITORS: DAVID JACKMAN & ROBIN SYDSERFF

PTMEDIA

CHRISTIAN
FOCUS

Copyright © Proclamation Trust Media 2008

ISBN 978-1-85792-790-0

10 9 8 7 6 5 4 3 2 1

Published in 2002
Reprinted 2008
by
Christian Focus Publications Ltd.,
Geanies House, Fearn, Ross-shire,
IV20 1TW, Scotland, Great Britain
with
Proclamation Trust Media,
Willcox House, 140-148 Borough High Street,
London, SE1 1LB, England, Great Britain.
www.proctrust.org.uk

www.christianfocus.com

Cover design by Moose77.com
Printed by Nørhaven Paperback A/S, Denmark

Contents

SERIES PREFACE

The *Teach the Bible* series is for preachers and Bible teachers. Few commentaries are written specifically with the preacher or Bible teacher in mind, and with the sermon or Bible study as the point of reference. The preacher or teacher, the sermon or talk, and the listener are the key 'drivers' in this series. The books are purposefully practical, seeking to offer real help for those involved in teaching the Bible to others. *Teaching John* was the first book published in the series and we are encouraged by the publication of a number of additional titles.

Our thanks, as ever, to the team at Christian Focus for their committed partnership in this project.

David Jackman and Robin Sydserff
Series Editors, London, March 2008

INTRODUCTION

For any Bible students, and for preachers in particular, John's Gospel is an inexhaustible treasure house. Throughout years of ministry, preachers will find themselves returning to it time and time again in order to proclaim its wonderful truths. So this book is designed to help and encourage Bible teachers of all kinds, but principally preachers who are preparing expository sermon series on books of the Bible, in rediscovering the spiritual riches that are in John's wonderful writing.

Teaching John is no more than a primer; it aims to open up the text for the Bible student and whet the appetite of the preacher. It is not an exhaustive exposition of the Gospel, far less a commentary on John. It is certainly not intended to take the place of the commentaries, as if these were unnecessary for the preacher. Quite the opposite; we try to point to helpful usage of these as we go along, and would encourage hard work on the text as a sine qua non of the preacher's preparatory task. But few commentaries seem to be written with the preacher and the congregation specifically in mind, and the sermon as the point of reference that is being worked towards. In this little book, then, as we work through selected portions of John's Gospel, these things – the preacher, the sermon and the congregation – will always be uppermost in our minds. The aim is to help the Bible teacher find a way into the text that will enable him to use it for its given purpose: to be preached. Whether we succeed or not is another matter, but we shall at least try!

We have limited ourselves to looking at John's stated key to understanding the reason why he wrote his book: the very familiar couple of verses at the end of chapter 20. Then we take this key in order to unlock four chapters – four very famous chapters (Ch. 3–6) – by way of example. Hopefully this will open up some fresh insights, and act as an incentive to further study of this magnificent fourth Gospel. All the time the sole aim is to be helpful to those engaged in the ministry of the Word.

I

THE KEY: EVIDENCE, FAITH & LIFE

> Jesus did many other miraculous signs in the presence of his
> disciples, which are not recorded in this book. But these are
> written that you may believe that Jesus is the Christ, the Son
> of God, and that by believing you may have life in his name.
>
> John 20:30-31

In these delightful words at the end of the main portion of
the Gospel, John the Apostle acknowledges that Jesus did a
multitude of other wonderful things as well as those he himself records. Indeed he did so many that all the libraries of the
world could not possibly contain them if written down! So,
inevitably John has decided to select, and this he does quite
drastically. He is not attempting to write a *Life*. He is not even
recording the whole public ministry; large tracts recorded in
the other Gospels are omitted. John's Gospel takes in about
twenty-one days in the earthly ministry of Jesus; twenty-one
days, mind you, of mighty works and even mightier words:
great claims, the carefully chosen 'I ams', great conversations
such as with Nicodemus and with the woman of Samaria.
So John confessedly selects, and with precise purpose. As
Ridderbos puts it, 'Here we have a highly concentrated
summary of the content and purpose of the fourth Gospel.'
But what is this purpose? Clearly this is a vital question if

we are to begin to pass on John's message today as faithful Christian teachers.

A Key to John's Book

When you look at these two verses (20:30-31), the simple order is as follows: first evidence, then belief, and then life. So, life is the ultimate goal; John's is a Gospel of life. But the only road to this life eternal is through faith in Jesus as God's only Son. And the only way to genuine Christian belief is through the first hand testimony of the apostles to their Lord and Saviour recorded in the sacred writings, the Scriptures. Let us look at each of these three key themes in more detail.

(1) Evidence

Clear and indisputable evidence is what John wishes to provide for his readers. Faith, for him, is no leap in the dark as some sceptics suppose it to be. Rather, as John 3:19-21 puts it, it is a step out of our darkness into that blinding light that exposes us for what we are.

What then are these Christian evidences?

They consist of the honest testimonies of honest men: testimonies to what they both saw and heard, touched and handled. Witness and testimony occupy a large part of John's Gospel, just as witness and testimony remain in all ages a vital means of establishing the truth of anything that has happened. Almost certainly at the very moment you read these words, men and women will be standing in the witness box somewhere, testifying under oath to what they saw and heard in relation to some alleged crime or incident, or some other investigation. The value of their witness depends not only on their integrity and truthfulness, but on whether they were actually present when the deed was done or the words spoken. So, it is with definite purpose that John affirms explicitly that the mighty signs and wonders he records were done *in the presence of Jesus' disciples*(30).

John's Gospel claims, then, with great clarity, to be verifiable history: an account of things that really happened. If not, then John's Gospel is a common fraud. On this particular territory terrific battles have been fought of course for nearly a century; all theological students know that, only too well. Fifty years ago we did not have the abundant help and backup that is available now, from the superb scholarly commentaries of Carson, Morris, Ridderbos, Beasley-Murray and others. But even so, many were never persuaded by liberal scholarship that we must yield on this point of the historicity of John's Gospel. There were plenty of reasons to be sceptical of the dogmatic statements made then by many scholars, when they reduced the fourth Gospel to a mere poem or a meditation, or declared that the raising of Lazarus was probably not intended to be taken literally. Looking back, how absurd many of those confident assertions now look! Indeed, the famous paper C.S. Lewis read to the theological students of Westcott House in the 1950s, subsequently published under the title *Fern-Seed and Elephants*, puts these 'assured results of modern scholarship' in their place with his customary devastating wit. It is arguably one of the finest things Lewis ever wrote, so one quotation is irresistible.

> Whatever these men may be as biblical critics, I distrust them as critics. They seem to me to lack literary judgment, to be imperceptive about the very quality of the text they are reading. It sounds a strange charge to bring against men who have been steeped in those books all their

lives. But that might be just the trouble. A man who has spent his youth and manhood in the minute study of New Testament texts and in other people's study of them, whose literary experience of those texts lacks any standard of comparison such as can only grow from a wide and deep and genial experience of literature in general, is, I should think, very likely to miss the obvious things about them. If he tells me that something in a Gospel is legend or romance, I want to know how many legends and romances he has read, how well his palate is trained in detecting them by the flavour; not how many years he has spent on that Gospel. But I better turn to examples.

In what is already a very old commentary I read that the fourth Gospel is regarded by one school of thought as a 'spiritual romance', 'a poem not a history', to be judged by the same canons as Nathan's Parable, the Book of Jonah, *Paradise Lost*, 'or more exactly *Pilgrim's Progress*'. After a man has said that, why need one attend to anything more he says about any other book in the world? [Isn't that a wonderful knock-out blow which would leave any boxer on the floor for good!] Note that he regards *Pilgrim's Progress*, a story which professes to be a dream and flaunts its allegorical nature by every single proper name it uses, as the closest parallel ... I have been reading poems, romances, vision-literature, legends, myths all my life. I know what they are like. I know that not one of them is like this. Of this text there are only two possible views. Either this is reportage ... pretty close up to the facts; nearly as close as Boswell. Or else, some unknown writer in the second century, without known predecessors or successors, suddenly anticipated the whole technique of modern, novelistic, realistic narrative. If it is untrue, it must be narrative of that kind. The reader who doesn't see this has simply not learned to read.[1]

We do not know what the students of Westcott House made of it, but ever since then people have been very grateful for that paper, which is worth-while reading for any Bible teacher or student for the ministry.

First then, is the evidence which is on the basis of first hand testimony. Carson is surely right to contend in his commentary that John's Gospel is primarily evangelistic in purpose. And John's evangelism has a clear apologetic basis. Like Paul (Acts 17:2-4; 18:4), John engages in reasoning, explaining, proving and persuading; and all this is in order that by God's grace his readers might believe.

(2) *Faith*
For John, as verse 31 makes clear, true faith involves believing certain things about Jesus, namely that he is none other than the promised Messiah, God's only Son, our Lord.

John's first aim was to evangelise Jews, Jewish proselytes and those God-fearing Gentiles attached to the synagogue. So he must demonstrate that the Christ is *this Jesus*, and no-one else. Now of course that is seldom our primary goal today in evangelism, unless we are engaged in gospel work in particularly Jewish communities. Most of us are preaching to Gentiles, increasingly not even God-fearers but to complete pagans, and our focus is normally to seek to show people that Jesus is the *Son of God*. While in origin this is a Messianic title, it ought to be understood here in John's Gospel in its full Christian sense, as it is so unmistakably in Thomas' great confession in John 20:28, ascribing Jesus the fullest deity. This is surely fundamental to John's aim from start to finish. Are not the very first words of his Gospel 'In the beginning

---

1. C S Lewis, *Fern-seed and Elephants and other essays on Christianity* (Glasgow, 1984), 107-108.

the Word was *God*' so significant, reminiscent as they are of the opening verses of Genesis? From the very beginning onwards, every part of his Gospel is intended to lead the reader to higher and higher views of Jesus of Nazareth, until the high watermark is reached in chapter 20, and *doubting* Thomas becomes *believing* Thomas confessing 'My Lord and My God!'. For John unless Jesus is our God, worshipped, adored and honoured, as we worship, adore and honour the Father, we do not have a Christian faith.

Once this underlying aim is grasped, many characteristics of the Gospel that we shall endeavour to draw out in the chapters that follow become so much clearer. Take for instance the recorded miracles. How very carefully they are selected to demonstrate that they are acts of creation. The stupendous raising of Lazarus – dead, buried, decomposing – is a supreme example, but all the other signs in John bear the same hallmark. For instance in chapter 9, the blind man is specifically said to have been born blind. This is not a story of sight ruined by disease and dirt (a common enough complaint of that day) now healed and restored by Christ's touch. No, here is a man that right from the womb had no original capacity to see. Here a creation miracle is needed; here the creator is at work, just as in chapter 6 he creates ample food for a vast multitude and walks upon the sea he has made, as though it is dry land.

But of course for John faith is much more than merely a clear conviction of truth. We are called also to believe *in* Jesus as verse 31 shows, to believe in his name, to put our whole trust in him, to come to him, to put our confidence in his word of promise. Of this we shall see more in the four chapters we study by way of example. Sufficient to say here that John is an expert, if we may so call him, on belief and unbelief. His Gospel abounds in brilliant cameos of faith, as well as brilliant illustrations and descriptions of refusal to believe. Why so many people of his day would not, could not, did not believe is, so to speak, his speciality. How devastating for instance, is John 5:44

> How can you believe if you accept praise from one another, yet make no effort to obtain the praise that comes from the only God?

Such a statement applies right across the spectrum, does it not – to the young person facing peer group pressure at school or college, to the theological scholar seeking acceptance in the academic world and in a hundred other ways in ordinary life?

John's great focus throughout the Gospel is on faith and unbelief as provoked by encounters with the person of Jesus himself.

(3) *Life*
But faith is the road to life: to eschatological life, eternal life, the life of the new age, the life of the world to come, yet anticipated now by life in the Spirit, a theme that John expounds so fully in his book. This life becomes ours right at the beginning, in the new birth by which we enter the Kingdom of God (3:5), and will become ours in all its fullness at the final resurrection. We shall see much more of this in our study of chapters 3–6, where we will discover that life is central to John's own proclamation of Jesus and his gospel in all four of these chapters in which he has recorded his own expositions for us.

The Key to Life

Life, the only true life, is the great goal. And for John, to bring to birth real knowledge and experience of this life among his readers and hearers is his overriding purpose. But such life is found in one place only: it is 'life in his name' (20:31, cf. 14:6). So belief, personal *faith* in the one and only God as made known in Jesus Christ, is the matter of crucial importance for John the evangelist. And belief is firmly grounded on *evidence*: the first hand testimony of those who saw, heard, and touched God the Saviour himself. The key to life, then, is the key to John's book.

2

THE KEY TO THE
RESURRECTION STORY

It will be useful now to take this three-dimensional key (evidence, faith, life) and see briefly how it unlocks John chapter 20, his account of the first Easter Sunday. This will serve as something of a test case, and an example for our studies to come. But as we do so, let us summarise the ground covered in chapter 1, in order to make quite sure we understand clearly John as an evangelist. Then we shall read what he writes with a clear sense of orientation towards his own stated purpose.

The person of Christ
First, we can say boldly that all John's gospel proclamation was *centred on the person of Christ*.

Note this even in these two little verses that we now know so well, 20:30-31. First, the signs that he is going to record are all miracles that Jesus did in the presence of his disciples. Second, the faith that John looks for is not just faith, or faith in God, but precisely faith in Jesus, that *he* is the promised Messiah and the Son of God from Heaven. And the life that may be ours? It is ours only in Jesus' name. We can receive it, we can have 'life in his name' by believing not on the church, not on the Holy Spirit, but on Christ himself. On his person, and his alone, we are to place our trust and pin our hopes. John's Gospel is Jesus centred, and ours must surely be the same.

The historical Christ

Secondly, we can say boldly of John the evangelist that the Christ he proclaims is the historical Christ.

He is not, for instance, the Christ of the church's experience or traditions, or our own experience or the experience of other people, rich as that may be. For this reason the growing trend to preach the gospel from the Gospels themselves, as well as from the rest of the New Testament, must be applauded. Many have certainly found this approach of great value in leading university missions, and many others in the many evangelistic courses now available that focus on the Gospels in particular. It is probably true to say that in the middle years of the twentieth century, evangelicals loved to preach the gospel chiefly from the epistles, especially Paul's letters. Of course the mighty Epistle to the Romans and the rest are powerful ammunition for the preacher and evangelist. Nevertheless, when Mark went into his study and began his famous book with those words, 'The beginning of the gospel about Jesus Christ, the Son of God' (Mark 1:1), the word *gospel* there does not mean book, as when we talk of giving someone a Gospel. That usage comes from the second century. No, he meant there the beginning of the *Good News*. Mark is consciously sitting down in his study to teach us the good news of Jesus Christ by his book. Expounding Mark, or John, is authentic gospel preaching, now as it was then. Of course that does not mean we should neglect preaching Christ from the epistles also. But it does certainly mean we must beware of drifting from the historical Christ, the Christ of Matthew, Mark, Luke and John. If we do that we shall find ourselves preaching another Jesus and another gospel, just like the pseudo-apostles in Corinth. The Christ of the four Gospels is the authentic Christ because he is the historical Christ by which every other 'version' of Christ must be measured.

John the preacher

Thirdly, we must say boldly that John the evangelist is not just a historian, a teacher or a most profound spiritual thinker, though he is all of these. He is first and foremost a preacher of salvation.

For John, Jesus is the Saviour of the world. For him, like his master, the fields are ripe for harvest. For him the urgent need of his Jewish religious contemporaries is the new birth. He preaches to a perishing world that God had sent his Son not to condemn but to save. And of course, so must we.

Seeing is Believing:
Evidence, Faith and Life in John chapter 20

Now, for a brief look at chapter 20, John's Easter Day chapter. How far does our key unlock its treasures? That is the question.

First and foremost, what stares us in the face in John 20 is evidence. It is the testimony of the disciple Jesus loved, the testimony of Mary Magdalene, the testimony of the Twelve (though now without Judas) and the testimony of

Thomas as well, all the more valuable because of course he had originally flatly refused to believe his fellow disciples and their excited account of meeting with Jesus back from the grave. The simple thrust of chapter 20 is not possible to miss: seeing was believing—that was the clear testimony of all of these characters.

The witnesses

First, as seems right and proper, John himself bears witness (3-9). He sees the grave clothes lying in the empty sepulchre, as though the body had passed through them without disturbing them (just as later that day Jesus will appear through closed and fastened doors). How different from poor old Lazarus staggering out encased and wrapped up like a parcel! Later there would be a fuller understanding for John, but for the moment, in the incomparable words of Charles Wesley,

> Vain the stone, the watch, the seal;
> Christ has burst the gates of hell:
> Death in vain forbids His rise;
> Christ has opened Paradise.

That is the testimony of John, the disciple Jesus loved.

Next, Mary Magdalene has her memorable meeting in the garden with the risen Jesus, and immediately goes off to the disciples with the straight-forward, but amazing, testimony: 'I have seen the Lord!' (10-18). Later that evening the disciples themselves are overwhelmed with joy when they too 'see the Lord' (20). He shows them his wounds in hands and side, his marks of identification. So this becomes their testimony to the absent Thomas: 'We have seen the Lord!' Only, from him they receive the response that Thomas had no intention whatever of believing such impossibilities, without tangible and incontrovertible evidence. And for that, apparently, he had no expectation; as far as he was concerned the dead simply do not return. But the rest of the story (24-29) goes on to recount how Thomas in fact did become what Acts 1:22 calls a witness of his resurrection: 'He saw the Lord'.

In short, John chapter 20 is packed full of evidence of the most compelling kind. It reminds us of the magnificent start of John's first epistle,

> That which was from the beginning, which we have heard, which we have seen with our eyes, which we have looked at and our hands have touched – this we proclaim concerning the Word of life. The life appeared; we have seen it and testify to it, and we proclaim to you the eternal life, which was with the Father and has appeared to us. We proclaim to you what we have seen and heard, so that you also may have fellowship with us. And our fellowship is with the Father and with his Son, Jesus Christ.
>
> 1 John 1:1-3

Three times here the proclamation is based upon first hand testimony, first hand evidence. It comes from honest men: seen, touched, handled and heard. John's decided emphasis is that his message is based on the surest foundation, on the strongest possible evidence.

Evidence leads to faith

What then of faith in John chapter 20? Well, we find that verse 29 gives us the grounds of faith very clearly.

> Then Jesus told him, "Because you have seen me, you have believed; blessed are those who have not seen and yet have believed."

For Thomas it was sight: clear, physical sight, with his own two eyes. For those who come after, when tangible evidence of the risen Christ will in the nature of the case not be provided, faith will, however, necessarily rest on the testimony of all those who did themselves witness the resurrection, and to whom the risen Christ did clearly appear physically (see 1 Cor. 15:6 for later appearances). Carson has an excellent note on verse 29, and aptly quotes 1 Peter 1:8-9. 'Though you have not seen him you love him, and even though you do not see him *now* you believe in him and are filled with an inexpressible and glorious joy ...'

The content of faith? Clear, incontrovertible evidence that convinces even the most unsentimental and down to earth of men. And here Thomas the erstwhile doubter is our teacher. It is on his confession, 'My Lord and my God!', that Arianism in all its forms must stumble and fall – whether held by today's Unitarians, or peddled by the persistent Jehovah's Witnesses. (Incidentally, an encounter with a Jehovah's Witness recently yielded from him the confident explanation of the meaning of Thomas' confession. It was, apparently, merely the shock of Jesus appearing in front of Thomas that caused him to respond by swearing: 'My God'! The human capacity to suppress the truth at all costs could hardly be more evident than in this kind of extraordinary reading of Scripture.)

Faith leads to life
Witness then led to faith. So, does faith lead to life in the same chapter? Indeed it does. We see it in the promise of the Holy Spirit given in verse 22, that John's readers post-Pentecost will already have heard of, and the church of his day already be experiencing. But the supreme expression of life in chapter 20 is of course the risen Lord himself, the central figure of the chapter. The picture we have before us is of Jesus of Nazareth now manifesting his glorified humanity. Here

is the proof that those who believe in him, though they die, will be raised imperishable, raised in glory, raised in power, raised a real, tangible spiritual body (1 Cor. 15:42ff).

This, the redemption of our bodies, is ultimately what the Christian indwelt by the Spirit eagerly awaits, though now we share in a frustrated, fallen and groaning creation. Tiresome theologians have often found only a realised eschatology in the fourth Gospel, collapsing all our future hopes into the present. This mistake is similarly evident when we Christian preachers, in order to attract our listeners overstate what is ours now in Christ – though truly that is rich indeed – and fail to explain the nature of Christian hope alongside Christian faith and Christian love. We give some space to deal with this in Chapter 6, where the issue surfaces clearly in the discussion of Jesus as the bread of life. Sufficient for now to show that our key, discovered in John 20:30-31 as evidence, faith and life (or testimony, belief and life, whichever you prefer) successfully unlocks the significance of John's resurrection chapter. The four sections of Peter and John (1-9), Mary Magdalene (10-18), the Twelve (19-23) and finally Thomas (24-29), are carefully chosen and recorded in order that hearers of John's message may come to believe that Jesus is the Christ, the Son of God, and that by believing they may have resurrection life in his name.

Now in chapter 20 it is perhaps no surprise to find a clear link between the chapter itself and the key verses that make up its conclusion. What is fascinating is that the same key unlocks many more chapters in John. It is beyond the scope of this book to deal with the whole Gospel. Nevertheless, we trust that giving some detailed attention to chapters 3, 4, 5 and 6 will serve as sufficient example for our purpose as a primer to whet the appetite for further study.

John's gospel is for preaching!

Our aim in this book is to be of some practical help to the Bible teacher. We want to inspire further thought and study of the text of John's Gospel, but always with a particular purpose in view: that of proclaiming the material as the very living word of God for men and women today. The Bible is meant to be preached! That is first and foremost the kind of 'thing' it is, and how it is meant to function. A car is made to be driven, not primarily to be polished. Pictures exist to be viewed, not just kept in a bank vault. So the Scriptures are given not to be pondered in the cloister, or the academy, but to be proclaimed as the word of the living, speaking God, by the preacher, for the church and to the world. We grapple with the message, then, not merely to understand it, but to pass it on.

So, the goal before us is to proclaim to others what John has himself been proclaiming to us as we have studied his Gospel, his own distilled exposition of *the* gospel of Jesus Christ. Before we leave this chapter, therefore, let us briefly think ahead to this next stage, and try to draw out how one might actually teach some of the material (or, perhaps better, think how we might, in our own words and expressions, re-preach what John has already preached for us in chapter 20).

We shall attempt, however sketchily, a sermon outline on one section of chapter 20. Hopefully it may serve as a catalyst to stimulate thinking on the rest of the chapter, and how it might be usefully broken up for preaching, perhaps as part of a series or as a mini-series on its own. There are of course numerous ways of taking this material for a sermon or Bible talk. Much would obviously depend on the context, the time available, and so on. One could certainly cover the whole of chapter 20 in one exposition, leading up to the great climax of verses 30-31, but it would be quite a tall order, and inevitably there would need to be selection.

Another useful way would be to take the four sections of the chapter (as conveniently paragraphed in the NIV) as four sequential messages, perhaps four Sundays after Easter, or four messages for a mission. What about something like this?

Seeing is Believing:
Four views on the Easter message

1. Two fishermen in an empty grave   (20:1-9)
2. A tearful woman in the garden   (20:10-18)
3. Fearful friends in an upper room   (20:19-23)
4. The hardened sceptic on the spot   (20:24-29)

A Tearful Woman In The Garden:
The Easter Message of Mary Magdalene

We shall take the appearance to Mary Magdalene in verses 10-18. In part this is provoked by a lively outline in a recent publication of the kind of book that aims to give preachers ideas for sermons throughout the church year. The comments and guide were for the principal service on Easter Sunday, so evidently this was meant to be an important and significant outline. Now, without doubt the spirit in which it was all written and prepared was of a thorough-going belief in the bodily resurrection and in the truthfulness of the story. There was no trace of heresy or unbelief. Nevertheless, the handling of the passage was startling, but perhaps all too common: not an example of collapsing the future into the present but of collapsing the past into the present. The historical situation is virtually bypassed altogether, presumably in an attempt to be contemporary and orientated to experience. The kind of approach taken was as follows:

The title of the outline is 'I have seen the Lord'. Fair enough (though one might ask who am "I"?). Then the sermon outline was divided into two main sections:

> In the first section was a statement to the effect that if we ask to be shown where Jesus is (as Mary asked) he will take *us* at our word and none of us will leave the empty tomb this morning as quite the people we were when we arrived.
>
> The second section suggests the message is that Jesus meets *us* this morning just as he met Mary – perhaps in an unexpected form: in a fellow worshipper, a child on the street, a stranger, a bus driver, doctor or lawyer or whoever. And as Jesus told Mary, so he tells us go and tell our brothers and sisters, and anyone who will listen, of the man who did not stay dead. Tell them of the wounds that survived a resurrection, and so on.

You can see that the ultimate thrust of this outline is that *we must go and tell as Mary was to go and tell.*

Now, despite all its undoubted liveliness, and much as we may heartily endorse the sentiment expressed, we must surely say that this way of handling the Bible is quite inadmissible. Everything that is said may be sound Christian truth. Without question, the message is clear Christian exhortation. But at most it is only an application (and hardly the main one) of the message of these verses. It is certainly far from being an exposition of the passage, because it fails to take seriously the stated purpose of John's writing; it fails to take seriously the fact that John is concerned with the historical Christ, with evidence, with witness, with the need to believe, and with the goal of life through faith in Jesus, the One and

Only, who is in the bosom of the Father, and who alone has made him known.

That is not for a moment to suggest that application is not necessary in our preaching; of course it is. As J I Packer has put it so well,

> preaching is teaching plus application (invitation, direction, summons); where the plus is lacking, something less than preaching occurs.[2]

But it is just as true to say that where the *teaching* is lacking, and the sermon is mere invitation, or direction, or summons, then something less than preaching occurs. And furthermore, exhortatory or devotional utterances of this kind are inevitably lacking in authority, because the link between the message being given and the Scripture that has been read is far from clear. In reality, the authority rests upon the reputation of the preacher himself, and his own attainment of learning in the eyes of the congregation. By contrast, when the application can be seen to flow clearly and unmistakably from the text in front of them, the hearers cannot help but see plainly that this is a word not from man, but from God, and that the authority is not from man, but from God. That is why expository preaching, that simply opens up the *message that is already there* in the text and applies it to the hearer, is so important today. We want people to be saying to themselves not 'what a learned preacher; for myself I can't see anything like that in today's passage', but rather 'Yes, I see that so clearly now – I can't believe I didn't see it before!'

Let us try to put this story in its historical setting, then, as in all integrity we must. And when we do, we shall find

---

2. 'Why Preach', *Honouring the Written Word of God*: The Collected Shorter Writings of J I Packer, Volume 3 (Carlisle: Paternoster, 1999), 249.

that we do not have to scratch around for application at all; it should actually become clear of its own accord as we begin to grasp what John is already saying. The task left to us is to say it again to our hearers, in language that is captivating and comprehensible to them.

One possible (and very basic) outline for consideration might be something like the following:

(1) Mary's Misery

After setting the scene, the main point is that Mary's acute misery was not in any way due to the fact that she could not find the *living* Jesus, but that she could not find his *corpse*. Evidently she had no expectations whatever of his rising on the third day. As far as holding on to any return from the grave – despite the story of Lazarus – Mary , it seems, can only be described here as an unbeliever. Like Thomas, she simply assumes that death is the end. No hallucinatory hopes here; she appears to be hopeless. Think of the abject misery we witness in crematoria and graveyards everywhere where there is no understanding of the reality of the true resurrection hope to be found in Jesus alone. It is the misery of those who grieve ignorantly, who have no hope; that is surely the point. (1 Thess. 4:13 might be a useful cross-reference here).

(2) Mary's Misunderstanding

Carson points out that verse 17 belongs to what he calls a handful of the most difficult passages in the Bible. (In that case, as we sometimes say to young preachers, it's a good thing you have started your preparation for Sunday on the Tuesday before!) Most modern commentators agree that Jesus is teaching Mary here that the old relationship is over. His comforting *physical* presence will no longer be accessible to his friends, as it has been for counsel and teaching previously. The future will be a matter of seeking him, but seated at God's right hand, (Col. 3:1-4). Instead of faith with sight, it will be necessarily a walk of faith *without* physical sight, albeit with his nearer spiritual presence through the promised Holy Spirit. Has he not been persistently telling his disciples that it is for their good that he is going away to the Father? And we too have to learn the sometimes difficult lesson of walking by faith in the Son of God who loved us and gave himself for us. We have to learn that to do so is in fact far better than were he still physically with us, and had not gone to his Father! The applications, surely, are legion.

(3) Mary's Message

Mary's messaage is not just 'I have seen the Lord'; it is more than just that 'the Lord is risen indeed!' It is the significance of him being risen. Notice in verse 17b she is told to tell them, 'I am returning to my Father and *your* Father, to my God and *your* God.' Look back to Chapter 14, and especially verses 2-3, where Jesus promised the disciples that he was 'going to prepare a place for you' (meaning through his death, though they did not grasp it then). So, through their Lord's return to heaven, the disciples will now have the inestimable privilege of sonship; they will be his brethren. Mark this key word implied by their shared paternity: not just disciples, they will be his brethren, sons of the same Father. From now on it is a matter of the shared privileges of sonship (the promise of 1:13 fulfilled). And what a message this is for weary sinners! Romans 8:15-16 and Hebrews 2:11-12 (citing Ps. 22) could be pondered fruitfully here, and one perhaps used as a brief cross reference in the sermon.

Much more could and ought to be said, but at least we can say that this is an honest attempt at handling a wonderful scriptural story. Without any straining or fanciful applications it is full of realism and relevance for today. There are messages about the factual reality of the resurrection itself. But there is much more also of the theological implications of the resurrection, in terms of the life of faith by the Holy Spirit, the wonder of the adoption accomplished through the cross that makes us sons of God, *born* of God, and the great hope of heaven. In other words, it is full of the good news of the gospel! What a great message there is here for any preacher to make much of on Easter Sunday, or any other day.

John has put into our hands a key to understand his book and the way he presents the gospel of Christ. This key very smoothly and efficiently unlocks the famous chapter 20. Next we shall discover how it unlocks the famous chapter 3 as well.

3

JESUS AND A DEVOUT
JEWISH CLERGYMAN

Now there was a man of the Pharisees named Nicodemus, a member of the Jewish ruling council. He came to Jesus at night and said, "Rabbi, we know you are a teacher who has come from God. For no one could perform the miraculous signs you are doing if God were not with him."

John 3:1-2

As we have seen, the twentieth chapter of John's Gospel majors on evidence for the resurrection of Christ in terms of those who were first hand witnesses of his new glory as the risen Lord. The final result was that even stubborn Thomas himself saw the Lord and as a result confessed his faith in Jesus, using the memorable words, 'My Lord and my God'. This is the high point of the Gospel of John. Jesus is now recognised not only as Messiah, but as very God of very God, to be honoured and worshipped as the Father in heaven is honoured and worshipped. Life, too, had its important place in chapter 20: Jesus sends the disciples on their new mission with the assurance of the power of the Holy Spirit. And in Jesus, the risen, living Saviour, they have a pattern of glorified humanity, a pledge of the resurrection life that will be theirs at his return.

So, with some confidence that John has put a key into our hands that will unlock much more of his book, we now set out to see how far the key helps us for the famous chapter 3, the dialogue between Jesus and a distinguished Jewish scholar, Nicodemus. The aim in these short studies is not, of course, to duplicate the excellent commentaries on John that are now available to a fortunate generation of preachers.[3] There are many details and many debated points we shall barely mention, since there is an adequate discussion of them in these books. Any preacher worth his salt will want to do – and must do – his own thorough-going verse-by-verse study, as he prepares a series on John's Gospel. This little book is no substitute for essential hard graft on the text in the study; indeed it is meant to stimulate it! Nevertheless, since the goal of understanding John's Gospel is to preach John's *gospel* (or re-preach his own preaching of the gospel), we need to find ways of handling the text with the specific aim of helping the preacher get from understanding the text to proclaiming the message, which is the end in view. This we shall try to do.

Our interest here is primarily in the shape, the remarkable structure, of each chapter. Often hardly noticed, it is a structure that John's key leads us to look for and to expect to find. Let us turn to this in John 3.

The 'key' elements in John chapter 3

If we take verses 1-2 as setting the scene, the subsequent material falls into three parts, recognisable in the NIV divisions, give or take a little: verses 3-8, 9-15 and 16-21.

When we examine these three sections separately we find that the main focus in each case comes from John's key – evidence, faith and life, or if you like, testimony, belief and life. What we discover is that part one majors almost exclusively on life, part two on testimony and part three on belief. Each part (of roughly similar size) is exceedingly

---

3. See chapter 9 for some brief recommendations among these.

compressed, but in spite of this, as Westcott points out, there is a distinct progress and completeness in the record and the order throughout is real and natural.

This simple structure is profoundly interesting. If the two key verses in chapter 20 demonstrate that John's Gospel is evangelistic in intent, then to find their ingredients reappearing openly in chapter 3 suggests that this chapter too is evangelistic in intent. What kind of evangelism do we find in chapter 3, then? We find the evangelism of the Jew, just as chapter 4 exemplifies the evangelism of the non-Jew. By the Jew, we mean the orthodox traditional Jew: a Pharisee and member of the Council, not today's liberal Jew who may be no different from any other ordinary, decent bloke, with only the vaguest religious ideas and no convictions whatever. Nicodemus is not that. He is a sincere man without condescension, and without undue cowardice; after all it was a fairly risky thing to come out at all to see Jesus. He was a kind of chief rabbi, a serious person and a scholarly one.

How do we evangelise people like that? It was certainly an urgent matter in John's day and it is still an important question today. Multiculturalism is bringing every religion under the sun into countries that were once thought of as 'Christian' nations. People are perhaps more religious than they have been for decades, with new syncretistic mixtures of religion abounding. Despite the atheism and agnosticism that is so much a part of western secularism, there are many people all around who have sincere and deeply held religious beliefs, who have some expectation of a life beyond the grave, and who are seeking for the truth about God. And of course, despite the decline in church attendance in countries like the United Kingdom, there are still many religious people, devoted to their church and all its traditions, but who have yet to come to grasp the reality of the personal gospel of Jesus Christ with all its implications and demands.

What makes this chapter so important is that it shows how the Lord himself sought to win for the truth just such a man with these special religious convictions.

God-centred, Trinitarian evangelism

Before plunging into part 1 to look at Nicodemus (vv. 3-8), it may help to give an overview of the whole, because evangelism too easily becomes man-centred or even church-centred, which is ultimately much the same. Here it is God-centred. Notice that Nicodemus is introduced first to the dynamic work of the Holy Spirit (3-8), then to the unique word and work of the Son (9-15), and then to the loving purposes of the Father (16-21) – in fact to the whole saving activity of the Triune God. What Nicodemus lacked was nothing less than the knowledge of the true God; what he needed was just that introduction to the Father which is ours only through a knowledge of Jesus as Lord. All this was to hang on the conversation that began that evening when a distinguished leader of the Jews sought to have an undisturbed meeting with the young rabbi, Jesus.

Life Has Come In Jesus, And Must Be Entered Into Now

> In reply Jesus declared, "I tell you the truth, no one can see the kingdom of God unless he is born again." [4] "How can a man be born when he is old?" Nicodemus asked. "Surely he cannot enter a second time into his mother's womb to be born!" [5] Jesus answered, "I tell you the truth, no one can enter the kingdom of God unless he is born of water and the Spirit. [6] Flesh gives birth to flesh, but the

Spirit gives birth to spirit. [7] You should not be surprised at my saying, 'You must be born again.' [8] The wind blows wherever it pleases. You hear its sound, but you cannot tell where it comes from or where it is going. So it is with everyone born of the Spirit".

John 3:3-8

It will be helpful to look at this section as a whole, and try to analyse what is going on in a kind of logical order. We shall pick out five main points that would help give some kind of shape to expounding this passage. It could be part of one message on the whole chapter, but there would be plenty here to fill out into just one message as part of a series of three (or more).

(1) *The Kingdom has come*
Notice that Jesus immediately introduces the theme of 'the kingdom of God'. Although common in the synoptics, it is found only here in John's Gospel (vv. 3 and 5) apart from an allusion in 18:36. Now this must alert the attentive reader. Why does he mention the kingdom of God? And what would it mean to Nicodemus? It would mean simply this: 'to participate in the kingdom at the end of the age, to experience eternal resurrection life' (Carson). That would be the hope of Nicodemus, as it is of course of many sincerely religious people in our own day. Jesus is making it clear that this hope is indeed a reality, and that it is a reality arrived in his own person. The kingdom has come.

(2) *Eternal life therefore begins now*
Jesus tells Nicodemus that if anyone is to participate in this eternal kingdom they must enter it here and now. The fact that this is so forcibly placed before Nicodemus right at the

start of the dialogue shows something of the priority Jesus placed upon this in his evangelism of his fellow Jews. It is no surprise to find John recording this, since it is characteristic of his Gospel to show that all God's great future blessings are in part anticipated now in this life – eternal life beginning not *after* death but at regeneration. But this challenging beginning also points to the reality that New Testament evangelism characteristically calls not for a discussion but for an immediate change. Think of John the Baptist's call for immediate repentance, and the same message preached by the Lord himself. Later in this chapter (3:18) we meet the same, where it is made clear that whoever fails to respond is condemned already. So, the pressing urgent need is the Spirit's work of regeneration, without delay: *now* is the day of salvation. See 2 Cor 6:1-2 for exactly the same emphasis in Paul's preaching, and, by implication, ours.

(3). *But God alone can regenerate*

What this exposes – to the shattering of human pride – is that by ourselves we are impotent to enter the kingdom of God. However privileged our birth, however religious or refined our nature, however pure our blood, however esteemed by others, however superior our achievements, entrance to God's kingdom is barred to us. Apart from a thorough-going regeneration, a creation act of God, making us a new kind of person altogether through a new kind of birth, we cannot enter the kingdom, or even see it (3,7). Therefore, in the words of Paul, there can be 'no confidence in the flesh' whatsoever (Phil. 3:4). That which is born of the flesh remains flesh, that which is born of the Spirit alone is spirit. God alone can impart life.

(4) This is the gospel of the Old Testament

This is vital to realise. Jesus clearly indicates that Nicodemus should not be surprised by this (7,10), because he, of all people, had known the gospel all his life. Did not the prophets of old repeatedly speak of a fundamental inner change? Of course they did! All the law ceremonies of the covenant spoke of this inner, spiritual reality right from the beginning (see Deut. 10:16; 30:6; Jer. 4:4; cf. Rom. 2:29), and increasingly the prophetic hope focused on the great full eschatological realisation of this for all peoples (Ezek. 11:19 ff.; 36:26 ff.; Isa. 44:3; Jer. 31:31 ff. are just some of the examples). But above all, Ezekiel 36:25-27 is surely the key to this conversation.

> I will sprinkle clean water on you, and you will be clean; I will cleanse you from all your impurities and from all your idols. [26] I will give you a new heart and put a new spirit in you; I will remove from you your heart of stone and give you a heart of flesh. [27] And I will put my Spirit in you and move you to follow my decrees and be careful to keep my laws ...

Jesus' reference to water in verse 5 cannot possibly be Christian baptism, or even to John's baptism. (If you need convincing, see Carson's[4] treatment of these verses which is excellent and comprehensive). To the unbiased reader of verses 3-8 it is clear that all the emphasis is on the work of the Spirit. It is this experience of the Spirit which includes two essentials, both pictured here: water and wind. On the one hand there is the experience of purification and cleansing from the old life (symbolised by water), and on the other the regenerating breath of the Spirit that brings the new life. (It

---

4. *The Gospel According To John* (Leicester: IVP, 1991), 191-196

is this latter, of course, that gives an answer to the question in the very next chapter from the one quoted, Ezekiel 37: 'can these dry bones live?') These two blessings are united in the new birth and are the promised blessings of the new covenant (Acts 2:38).

It is worth noting, therefore, that there is continuity here with the Old Testament, but there is also contrast. Here is something foretold by the prophets, and anticipated in the experience of the Old Testament saints prospectively. Yet it is fully realised in the experience of God's people only after the death, resurrection and ascension of the Lord Jesus Christ. 'This is the gospel you have in your own Bible' Jesus is telling Nicodemus. 'This is the gospel of Abraham, and Moses, and David. But you obviously have never grasped it and really believed, or else you would have been expecting me, and you would believe in me right now, today!' (cf John 5:43; 7:19,23). There has only ever been one gospel.

(5) Jesus is the only way
This has already become clear in passing, but is very evident in this Nicodemus dialogue and so important to highlight today. This new birth is not optional. 'You must be born again' insists Jesus to Nicodemus (7), for no-one – no-one – can see the kingdom of God otherwise. Such emphatic denials are very characteristic of John's style in his Gospel throughout, and surely must be an echo of the Lord's method of teaching. This must be impressed upon all of us who wish to be honest preachers of the truth. People require more than positive preaching in these days of relativism and post-modernity, just as they did in the first century (or any century, for that matter). For Jesus, it was necessary to state the logical consequences of the positive teaching. It was not enough to

teach, for example, that he was the way, the truth and the life, (14:6a) without adding that no-one could come to God except through him (14:6b): in other words, that there was no other way to God, no other truth about God, no other life experience of God except through him. So it is here in John 3. It is a lovely thing to preach verse 18a, for example: there is no condemnation now for those who believe now. But the preacher must also spell out verse 18b: that those who fail to believe in Jesus now are, here and now, under the condemnation and wrath of God. This surely is what makes a faithful preacher.

So much then for section one of Jesus' conversation with Nicodemus (3-8), even though much more might be said. To summarise: Jesus confronts the great teacher in Israel with the fact that the kingdom has already arrived in himself. That eternal kingdom is to be entered and enjoyed now by the work of God's Spirit, prophesied in the very Scriptures Nicodemus treasured and taught: 'I will sprinkle clean water on you and you will be clean. I will give you a new heart and put a new spirit in you.' It is as though Jesus is saying, 'Nicodemus do you know this for yourself – not just in your head, but in your mind, and heart and soul? Nicodemus, the promised time has come. That life, the new covenant life, has come in me and must be entered into now.'

Jesus Himself Is The Supreme Witness To God

"How can this be?" Nicodemus asked. "You are Israel's teacher," said Jesus, "and do you not understand these things? [11] I tell you the truth, we speak of what we know, and we testify to what we have seen, but still you people do not accept our testimony. [12] I have spoken to you of

earthly things and you do not believe; how then will you
believe if I speak of heavenly things? [13] No one has ever
gone into heaven except the one who came from heaven
— the Son of Man. [14] Just as Moses lifted up the snake
in the desert, so the Son of Man must be lifted up, [15] that
everyone who believes in him may have eternal life.

John 3:9-15

Remember that this section focuses on testimony, evidence.
The best evidence for the ministry of Jesus is the person
of Jesus himself, his words and his works. Nicodemus has
already felt the force of both. Recall verse 2, where he said,
'We know you are a teacher who is come from God'. He is
already struck by Jesus' words and his teaching, and went on
to say, 'No-one could perform the signs you do, the miracles
you do if God were not with him.' So Nicodemus has already
been affected by the words and works of Jesus, which are of
course the evidence which brings people to Jesus, and to a
knowledge of God. What now confronts Nicodemus, and
us when we read this section, is the Lord's own testimony to
the ultimate source of both his words and his works. Already
we know that testimony to the truth is a major theme of
this Gospel. And the nature of this testimony is that of a
truthful witness, bearing first-hand testimony to what he has
personally seen and heard. What is so dramatic here is that
Jesus now bears direct testimony before this learned Jew to
a non-mediated knowledge of the invisible God, the Father
in heaven, which he, Jesus, uniquely possesses. A glance at
verses 11-13 is of great importance.

Unique testimony from the heart of heaven itself (11-13)
It is a pity to be distracted (as many commentators are)
by the 'We' of verse 11. It could be a response to the 'We'

that Nicodemus uses in verse 2, but what it cannot be is a
reference to his band of disciples. For Jesus is testifying here
to what he *alone* has seen. He is echoing the great words of
1:18: 'No-one has ever seen God; but the One and Only,
[himself] God, who is in the bosom of the Father, has
made him known' (a valuable cross-reference here). This is
something far beyond the 'I have seen' of chapter 20. There,
the disciples can say that they have seen the Lord raised from
the grave to a new order of being. Here, by contrast, Jesus
claims to have seen the one called 'God the blessed and only
ruler, the king of kings and Lord and Lords who alone is
immortal and lives in unapproachable light whom no-one
has seen or can see' (1 Tim 6:15-16). The tragedy, still as
much a tragedy in modern Judaism as then, is spelt out in
the sad words that follow, 'but still you people do not accept
our testimony'. Plummer, whose valuable little Cambridge
commentary (now over a century old) can still be found
second hand, calls this 'the tragic tone in John's Gospel'. This
tragic tone begins to sound as early as the prologue:

> He was in the world, and though the world was made
> through him, the world did not recognise him. He came
> to that which was his own, but his own did not receive
> him.
>
> John 1:10-11

In many ways the whole of the first half of the Gospel is taken
up with expounding these verses and their theme of Jewish
unbelief, before in the second half John turns to expounding
what it means to be those who have received him, who believe
in his name, and are given the right to become children of
God (1:12).

But here, 3:12 carries on the tragedy, the supreme tragedy,
of Jewish unbelief. Perhaps the 'earthly things' mentioned

here refer to Jesus' parables of birth and wind earlier in the conversation, which Nicodemus did not fathom. More likely it refers more widely than that, to the many situations where Jesus has spoken to all the Jewish leaders – of their empty traditions, their puzzling tragedies (Luke 13:1), their false hopes – and on every occasion has not been believed. As for the 'heavenly things', in the context here these must refer to the divine counsels respecting man's salvation, which immediately follow in verse 14, and in the great third section (16-21). Westcott, (whose old commentary is still worth gold despite its sacramentalism and other oddities), has a valuable note on verse 13, 'No-one has ever gone into heaven except the one who came from heaven, the son of man'. This does not imply that Christ has ascended to heaven as though he were one of a class, and is here contrasted with all the others, as better and higher. Rather, the point is that he alone enjoyed that directness of knowledge, by his very nature, which another could only attain to by such an ascension.

These three verses are very remarkable, and make unique and extraordinary claims for the testimony of Jesus himself. But such statements occur right through John's Gospel. Look on to 3:31 where we read

> The one who comes from above is above all; the one who is from the earth belongs to the earth, and speaks as one from the earth. The one who comes from heaven is above all. He testifies to what he has seen and heard, but no-one accepts his testimony.

Or think of chapter 8, which is particularly rich in these astonishing statements. Jesus can say:

> I have much to say in judgment of you. But he who sent me is reliable, and what I have heard from him I tell the world' … I do nothing on my own but speak just what

the Father has taught me ... You are determined to kill
me, a man who has told you the truth that I heard from
God.

John 8:26,28,40

There is a further exceptionally clear verse in 12:50 'I know
that his command leads to eternal life. So whatever I say is just
what the Father has told me to say.' And finally, the remarkable
negative and positive of 6:46, 'No-one has seen the Father
except the one who is from God; only he has seen the Father.'

Jesus' testimony is unique. He brings unmediated revelation from the highest heaven, from God the Father himself.
The words of his testimony are unique revelation, and his
own person is unique revelation: unique testimony from the
heart of heaven itself.

The message from the heart of heaven is the message of the cross (14-15)

Jesus speaks of what he, and he alone, knows of the divine
counsels, the 'heavenly things'. This refers to verses 14 and 15,
though at first sight these verses seem to make an abrupt
change of subject. But it is to his own works that Jesus refers.
He came down from heaven to tell us the truth about God
who made us, but also to live and die that we might ourselves
know the God who so loved this sinful and stricken world
that he gave his only son to redeem it.

It is notable that all this is introduced to Nicodemus
in Old Testament terms, by the famous story of the brass
serpent (Num. 21:8 ff.) The meaning is clear: the lifting up
of a source of life which becomes effectual through the faith
of the helpless sufferer. Nicodemus lived to see with his
own eyes the fulfilment of this prophecy (19:39). It was by
his words, his teaching, yes, but above all by his work, his

death, that Jesus bore direct witness to the truth of God's immeasurable love. For John in his Gospel it is the death of Jesus that is his exaltation, his glory *par excellence*, his return to the Father. And this remains to this day supremely the ground of Christian faith. It was then for Nicodemus; it is now for us. It is by Jesus incarnate and crucified and risen that light came into the world.

We must not miss that John's further record suggests Nicodemus did indeed bravely come into the light (7:50; 19:39). Surely we are meant to take special note of this. Later, in chapter 3, we have John's testimony that

> The one that comes from heaven is above all. He testi-
> fies to what he has seen and heard but no-one accepts
> his testimony. The man who has accepted it has certified
> that God is truthful. For the one whom God has sent
> speaks the words of God; to him God gives the Spirit
> without limit.'
>
> John 31-34

Nicodemus is one who did, at last, apparently accept Christ's testimony and so certified that God is truthful. He seems to have been that rare exception in the Judaism of his day. Thankfully there are still exceptions to Jewish unbelief and for every such Jewish conversion to Christ today we give thanks to God, though we must surely pray and work for more.

Jesus' testimony, his words and his work, is evidence of a unique nature. It is a message direct from heaven, direct from God himself. Yet, it was rejected, for the most part, even by those who were 'his own folk'. They were maddened by his words, and scandalised by the word of his cross, just as people are today. But whatever the reaction of men, this truth remains for ever: Jesus himself is the supreme witness to God.

It is The Responsibility of All To Believe In Jesus

For God so loved the world that he gave his one and only Son, that whoever believes in him shall not perish but have eternal life. [17] For God did not send his Son into the world to condemn the world, but to save the world through him. [18] Whoever believes in him is not condemned, but whoever does not believe stands condemned already because he has not believed in the name of God's one and only Son. [19] This is the verdict: Light has come into the world, but men loved darkness instead of light because their deeds were evil. [20] Everyone who does evil hates the light, and will not come into the light for fear that his deeds will be exposed. [21] But whoever lives by the truth comes into the light, so that it may be seen plainly that what he has done has been done through God.

John 3:16-21

Most modern commentaries take verses 16-21 to be John's words by way of further explanation of his Lord's message for Nicodemus. Some go on to note that monologue rather than dialogue began back in verse 11. It matters not, since the Spirit's superintendence of holy Scripture means that the promises of John 14:26 and 16:13 are being fulfilled in John's writing, guaranteeing the accuracy of this third and final section. It is obvious to the reader that there is a seamless join between verse 15 and 16; the theme of believing in Jesus has been introduced (15) and is now fully explored in verses 16-21.

Belief and unbelief in the Triune God
As we approach a section of Scripture that has meant so much to millions of Christian believers, let us be clear that

the purpose here is not to expound fully these verses so much as to examine the section in the light of our key to John's Gospel. So far section one majored on life, section two on testimony. If John is to be consistent with his declared purposes the third and final section will major on faith: on belief and unbelief. This is precisely what it does. Everything is concentrated on the importance of believing. Verse 18 is a good example:

> Whoever believes in him is not condemned, but whoever does not believe stands condemned already because he has not believed in the name of God's one and only Son.

At this point we recall John's Trinitarianism, a characteristic that stands out here, as it does in chapter 4. We have heard of the work of the Spirit, or rather Nicodemus has. (We must not forget him or we lose the historical context of this chapter). Next in section two all the focus was on the work of the Son as revealer and redeemer, both revealing by his words and redeeming by his work. Now the centre of attention is the loving plan of God the Father and sender of the Son for the salvation of the world. The work of the Spirit, the work of the Son, the work of the Father in our salvation are inseparable (though never confused) in John's presentation of the gospel. It must be a pattern for ours also.

God's love for a rebellious, lost world

The vast scope of the divine love is first signalled in verse 15; the Son of Man is to be lifted up, in order that – mark the word – *everyone* who believes in him may have eternal life. And so it continues. God so loved the world, wicked in rebellion and perishing as it is, that whoever believes in Jesus shall not perish (16); whoever believes in him is not condemned (18).

All this of course is totally unexpected as far as a member of the Jewish council is concerned. It is worse than that, for we are told plainly that God did *not* send his Son into the world to condemn the world, richly though that condemnation is and was deserved. This must have been a terrible shock to Nicodemus and others of his ilk.'In the later Jewish messianic anticipations the judgment of the nations by Messiah is the most constant and the most prominent feature' (Westcott). However, as Nicodemus now hears in these astonishing words, God sent his Son not to condemn but to *save* the world. Again, Westcott has a fine way of putting things:

> The divine purpose in the incarnation is one of universal love even though it was imperfectly realised by man, a purpose of life for the believer, of salvation for the world.[5]

There are of course theological issues and difficulties regarding the whole question of the love of God, the problem of evil, righteous judgment and so on. Such issues require extended discussion beyond the scope of this book. Don Carson has written very freshly and persuasively on these problems, and we happily commend his recent little book on the subject.[6]

So then, we shall take verses 16-21 as a whole, and select two points only. In a series of addresses on John 3 it would be quite in order for one sermon to major on just these two things, so as to develop them adequately. (There is no need always to rush through huge chunks of the text in one go. Even sermon cards can be amended if you discover that you need an extra week to do the passage justice; the church will not collapse if you do!)

---

5. *Gospel of St John* (John Murray, 1882), 55.
6. *The Difficult Doctrine of the Love of God* (Leicester: IVP, 2000), a provocative title and a most encouraging study.

(1) *Personal responsibility to believe the gospel*

John has no hesitation in emphasising human responsibility in this record of the Lord's teaching and practice. Equally clearly later on we shall see him teaching divine freedom and sovereignty (as he does in 3:8). But here the emphasis is firmly on the listener's responsibility to believe. The Lord himself looked for a definite response of faith in his claims: to take him at his word and trust in his promises. He called on his hearers immediately to accept his testimony and take him at his word. Moreover, not to believe in him would have momentous consequences: it deserved and received divine condemnation. There is therefore a clear sense in this section that a person's destiny is in their own hands. To refuse God's one and only Son and his sacrifice is to refuse the one and only way of salvation. It is to reject life and settle for darkness and death (cf. 36). It is well worth reading through these six verses again with this in mind noting how clearly human activity for good or ill is underlined. We should not miss this. True, the final twist in verse 21 safeguards prevenient grace; nevertheless, in verses 19-21 the spotlight is on human deeds. What is of supreme importance in this section is what men and women do with the light they receive.

Nicodemus was beginning to realise that this meeting with Jesus was more, much more, than a brilliant tutorial. If what he was hearing was true then he faced a big personal decision: could he conceivably commit himself to Jesus and his ministry? Or should he return to the darkness from which he came? The position of neutral observer was clearly untenable: it was salvation or condemnation. From the very start new life had been put before him as an urgent necessity. Must we not then take it that this was a characteristic of Jesus as an evangelist? The synoptics support this same pattern:

> After John was put in prison, Jesus went into Galilee,
> "The time has come," he said. "The kingdom of God
> is near. Repent and believe the good news!" As Jesus
> walked beside the Sea of Galilee, he saw Simon and
> his brother Andrew casting a net into the lake, for they
> were fishermen. "Come, follow me," Jesus said, "and I will
> make you fishers of men." At once they left their nets and
> followed him.
>
> Mark 1:14-18

This is the picture we get of Jesus preaching the Gospel.
And this we must add: for him and his Jewish contemporaries in particular, the crisis had come. For them the
future held either belief or growing hardness of heart and
alienation from God. That is what John charts out for
us throughout his Gospel. The first point then concerns
human responsibility. This section is full of it and we
should learn from it.

(2) *Responsibility to tell of the gospel*

Though not so explicitly stated in this section as the first
point, this second conclusion seems inevitably to follow
from it. Along with human responsibility to believe in Jesus
comes Christian responsibility to tell about Jesus. Jesus
himself exemplifies this God-given responsibility to go first
to his own people, to the lost sheep of the house of Israel.
But if his God-given mission was also to save the world, then
completely new horizons of responsibility are opened up.
Judaism has never been a missionary faith, whereas Christ's
word is for everyone in the whole wide world. John's book
then, like this chapter, is evangelistic in intent. But those who
believe are immediately made aware of what their mission
is, as are the post-resurrection believers (20:20-23). As the
Father sent Jesus, so he is sending them.

But as well as challenge, there is great encouragement here. This third chapter contains two characteristic Johannine emphases that give strength and reassurance to us in our evangelism as we seek to go out into all the world. First, the reiteration in John 3 (as indeed throughout his book) of mankind's refusal to accept the message. If that was so with Jesus the evangelist, it will be so with us. This important warning will deliver us from despair and discouragement in Christian outreach. Not that human rejection is entirely negative in the New Testament; for example in the Acts the repeated refusal of God's ancient people to accept the gospel was indication to the apostles that they must move out into the harvest field of the Gentile nations. As Paul says in Acts 28:28 'they will listen.'

Secondly, God so loved this big bad world that he sent his Son into this world. His purpose is to save the world. As John 1:9 puts it, the true light that lightens every man was coming into the world. With this extraordinary vision before us we can never become discouraged, whatever individual setbacks we may have. If such is the divine purpose, it is certain that an uncountable number from every nation, tribe, people and language in the world will one day gather before the throne of God to give praise to their redeemer. Who can estimate the grains of sand on the seashore or the number of stars in the infinite universe as it is now thought to be?

In regard to this, it is interesting to see how the great nineteenth-century Reformed theologians of Princeton saw matters. There is a fascinating insight into this in Charles Hodge's writing at the very end of his *Systematic Theology*. He is dealing with an issue that is much debated today, even in evangelical circles – future punishment and its duration – and his final words are solemn enough:

> We should be constrained to humility and to silence by
> the fact that the most solemn and explicit declarations of
> the everlasting misery of the wicked fell from the lips of
> him who, though equal with God, was found in fashion
> as a man, and humbled himself unto death, even death
> on a cross, for us men and for our salvation. [7]

This is well said, and undoubtedly clear biblical truth, however unpopular it may appear today. However, in speaking
faithfully and plainly about the horror of eternal judgment,
he is nevertheless careful to follow the biblical pattern of
doing so only in the context of the surpassing wonder of the
great and expansive salvation in the glorious gospel of Christ.
God's great over-riding purpose is not to condemn, but to
save! The Reformed preacher and theologian of all men has
large convictions about the fulfilment of the great divine
purposes because he has large conceptions of the greatness
and glory of God. And so just before the above, Hodge can
write these remarkable words:

> We have reason to believe that the number of the
> finally lost, in comparison with the whole number of
> the saved, will be very inconsiderable. Our blessed Lord
> when surrounded by the innumerable company of the
> redeemed will be hailed as the Saviour of men, as the
> Lamb that bore the sins of *the world*. [8]

We may hesitate to be so bold as he concerning the specifics
of the relative number of those saved and lost; Scripture
does not seem to put it in exactly these terms – though
may it indeed be so, for God's glory! But surely the thrust
of what he is saying is just what John is proclaiming to us

---

7. Charles Hodge, *Systematic Theology Vol. 3* (Grand Rapids: Eerdmans,
1982), 880.

8. *Systematic Theology*, 879-80.

here in this great third chapter: God is a saving God, and his great purpose for a lost, rebellious world is a purpose of grace and salvation, boundless and free. Jesus is the Saviour of the world!

4

JESUS AND A TAINTED WOMAN

In John 3:1-21, which might not unreasonably be called how a chief rabbi was won for Christ, it became clear that the story was indeed structured round the three 'key' elements of John 20:30-31: testimony, belief and life. The order, however, was life, testimony and belief, and in fact this order is true to what we find in everyday life and experience. First comes the work of the Holy Spirit in regenerating power. Everything begins with this divine initiative, for it is God alone who awakens the deadened heart and the conscience in the complete unbeliever. This is followed by recognition – which may of course be sudden or gradual – that it is Jesus, and Jesus alone, who speaks uniquely of heavenly things because of his first hand witness, his direct revelation from the presence of God. Then this dawning light is what brings someone to conscious faith in Jesus, to coming fully into the light and receiving the verdict of no condemnation (John 3:18, 5:24).

Evangelism and God's sovereignty

What is so striking is that if the first section (3:3-8) illustrated divine sovereignty and freedom in grace, section three (3:16-21) illuminated the absolute necessity of human responsibility. These two extremes seem to us to be in conflict, and may appear contradictory. Of course there has been endless theological debate, not to say argument and extreme disagreement, among believers over the way to reconcile and explain such difficulties, and here is not the place to enter a long digression on the subject. However, we should notice that for John (and indeed for the other New Testament writers) there appears not a trace of difficulty in giving equal weight and importance to both the sovereign grace of God and the clear responsibility of man to respond to the gospel summons. Both are clearly emphasised, and indeed often juxtaposed in a striking way with no sense of embarrassment whatsoever (see for example 6:29, 37ff). So Charles Simeon seems to hit the nail on the head in a most practical way for the Bible teacher, in saying that we should not strive to see the 'real' truth as being found in one extreme, or in the other extreme, or in a balance midway between; we should recognise the biblical reality that the truth is in fact to be found fully in both extremes! Neither can be omitted from the scheme of salvation as we know it in the New Testament, and neither must be omitted from our preaching of that salvation. But the joy of expository preaching that is governed by the flow of the biblical books as they stand before us is that if we expound the text faithfully, weighing it as the writer weighs it, and emphasising what he emphasises for us, we can be confident that we are not putting asunder what God has joined together. Rather, we shall indeed be 'unashamed workmen, rightly handling the word of truth' (2 Tim. 2:15), not getting stuck perpetually on our own particular hobby horses. This will be a great salvation for us, and for our congregations!

The 'key' in John 4

Now it is time to ask ourselves whether in chapter 4 the pattern of the 'key' is operative in the section which makes up the account of the conversion of many Samaritans (1-42). As we consider this marvellous conversation at Jacob's Well and its astonishing result, it is impossible not to be struck by the wealth of Christian teaching that is to be found here. From John 4 many sermons and talks have been quarried on the range of rich themes we find here: on the possibility of satisfying our spiritual thirst, on patterns of personal work, on true worship that is in spirit and truth, on the harvest field and the urgency of the evangelistic message, and many more. All this is certainly legitimate. We must not forget that there are multitudes of ways to preach and apply the unsearchable riches of Christ from the Scriptures. New light continues to dawn, and will do so, for the Word of God is an inexhaustible treasure house always yielding new treasures as well as old. But here we must largely set these aside for the sake of our particular focus, namely to demonstrate that John is using his familiar schema here as elsewhere, thus revealing the great importance he thinks it has in gospel work and preaching. So in this chapter we shall take the original order of the 'key' elements of 20:30-31: testimony, faith and life, and locate these where they come in the narrative, rather than taking the verses in chronological order, as we did in chapter 3.

Testimony To The One True Saviour Of The World

In this conversation with the Samaritan woman there are two records of witness, or testimony. First the testimony of the Samaritan woman (27-30, 39) then the testimony of the Samaritan townspeople (40-42). Let us work backwards, and deal first with the testimony of the Samaritan townspeople.

The talk of the whole town

> Many of the Samaritans from that town believed in him because of the woman's testimony, "He told me everything I ever did." ⁴⁰ So when the Samaritans came to him, they urged him to stay with them, and he stayed two days. ⁴¹ And because of his words many more became believers. They said to the woman, "We no longer believe just because of what you said; now we have heard for ourselves, and we know that this man really is the Saviour of the world."
>
> John 4:39-42

At first, we are told, it was because of the woman's testimony that they believed in Jesus. According to the record they believed sufficiently to leave Sychar and come out to Jacob's Well, where Jesus was, in order to press the Lord to stay with them. He did so for two days, and the result of this wonderful time of investigation and teaching is given in verse 42 'we have heard for ourselves'. So here testimony leads to belief: to clear convictions that Jesus is none other than the *world's* Saviour, the truly tremendous theme we met in John 3:17.

We shall not dwell long on the townspeople, but do note that their testimony to Jesus is based upon seeing him and hearing him for themselves. Indeed that is the very language they use; that is how they come to know the truth that Jesus really is the Saviour of the world. All this implies that central to the teaching that the Lord gave to the Samaritans during those two days was his claim to be not just the Messiah of narrow Jewish expectations, indeed not that at all, but the world's redeemer. What astonishing news that must have been to hear! But it is still this world's only hope, and the ground of all our hopes for the triumph of the gospel.

This does not mean universalism, of course: that everybody is going to be saved at the end. Nor does it mean that we need entirely echo Charles Hodge's words, quoted at the end of the last chapter. (Driven by powerful eschatological expectation, these men were seeing the enormous missionary expansion of the nineteenth century, and it seemed to them that the imminent conquest of the world for Christ was a real possibility.) The fact is that we are given no specific answer in Scripture as to how many or how few will ultimately be saved, except that it shall certainly be a multitude that no man can number! Rather, the emphasis in the Bible is not speculative, but practical. We are urged by Jesus to take heed, and enter personally into his kingdom now before it is too late. Meanwhile we hold on to the tension of the two realities announced in chapter 3: on the one hand God so loved the world and sent his Son to save the world, and on the other the reality that mankind hates the light and loves the darkness, something of which we today are all too well aware after the twentieth century.

The talk with a sinful Samaritan woman

> Then, leaving her water jar, the woman went back to the town and said to the people, [29] "Come, see a man who told me everything I ever did. Could this be the Christ?"

³⁰ They came out of the town and made their way toward
him …. Many of the Samaritans from that town believed
in him because of the woman's testimony, "He told me
everything I ever did."

John 4:28-30,39

So we turn now to the testimony of the Samaritan woman.
At first sight this testimony 'Come, see a man who told me
everything I ever did' may seem a little thin. Yet, this is far
from the truth. She is in fact making a very great claim
fraught with associations for the discerning reader. John is
very fond of allusions like this, which would immediately
evoke Scriptural themes in the minds of his primarily Jewish
audience. Compare her testimony here with, for example,
that of Nathaniel in 1:47ff. In answer to his question 'How
do you know me?' Jesus answered 'I saw you while you were
still under the fig tree before Philip called you.' Nathaniel, a
godly believing Jew, immediately declared in response 'Rabbi,
you are the Son of God, you are the king of Israel.' Clearly to
Nathaniel, this claim of Jesus to have known all about him
before ever he had met him spoke powerfully of a claim to
be someone very special indeed. Why? Well, just think of
the amazing words of Psalm 139,

> O LORD, you have searched me and you know me.
> ² You know when I sit and when I rise; you perceive my
> thoughts from afar. ³ You discern my going out and my
> lying down; you are familiar with all my ways. ⁴ Before a
> word is on my tongue you know it completely, O LORD.
> (Ps. 139:1-4)

Here then is the God from whom no secrets are hid; that
is the staggering testimony here! Here is the LORD himself,
who knows without being told about this woman's murky
and miserable past, about her deep need for that living water

that alone can satisfy her, about the time that is soon to come when worship in Jerusalem and on Mount Gerizim will be irrelevant, and about everything else.

No doubt we could enlarge on the significance of the woman's testimony 'He told me everything I ever did'. However, it seems that what matters much more than these words is the person who spoke them. This is at the heart of the drama being played out that day and this is at the heart of John's message to us. So who is this person? The answer to this question is what enables us to grasp the divine revelation Jesus brought into the world that is recorded here. First, we have in this person a Samaritan. Second, we have in this person a woman. Thirdly, we have in her a sinner whose guilt is beyond doubt. Grasp these three things and we come much closer to understanding what it means for Jesus to be the world's Saviour, since the Jewish establishment of the day would have held some things at least as plain and self-evident about when Messiah came: that he would have nothing to do with Samaritans, women or self-condemned sinners!

(1) Jesus came to save even the religious ignorants of this world
First, then, Jesus meets a Samaritan. The significance of this can be found in any good Bible dictionary. In a very brief potted history, we can sum it up as follows. Samaria was captured by the Assyrians long centuries ago. Large numbers of inhabitants were deported and replaced by all sorts and conditions of people from the Assyrian empire, the story of which is told in 2 Kings 17:24. As a result of this, to the worship of the God of Israel was now added the worship of the gods of the pagan newcomers, and for many centuries the people of Samaria had a multi-cultural and multi-faith society. There was a great deal of hostility between them

and the Jews who returned from Exile (cf. Ezra 4:2, 9-10), but wonderfully, despite all this, the worship of the true God did survive, though it was a truncated faith based on the Pentateuch only, and of course without a true centre of worship, as Jesus makes very clear in his answer to the woman's question in verse 22. The temple that the Samaritans built on Mount Gerizim around 400 BC was burned by the Jews in 128 BC, and much more could be added to explain the bitter feelings and the deep hostility between Jews and Samaritans. In Carson's words the Jews would regard the Samaritans as 'children of political rebels, racial half-breeds whose religion was tainted by various unacceptable elements'[9]. Tainted is perhaps too soft a word; poisoned might be better. Yet for this Samaritan Jesus our Lord purposefully came.

Older devotional writers and preachers made much of verse 4, especially in the old translation, 'He must needs go through Samaria', as though this was an unusual route. However, scholars think it likely that Jesus was not necessarily going off the normal route for his journey, and that all but the most fastidious Jew would go through Samaria just this way. Nevertheless, the old preachers were right. This journey was not by chance, and John clearly draws attention to this. Jesus, as ever, is in perfect step with his Father. There is not the slightest doubt that this encounter with Samaritans was in the plan and purpose of God. It is a taste, an anticipation of the future now very close at hand, a future changed forever for all peoples through the imminent climax of the redeeming work of Christ the Saviour.

It is Acts 1:8 that gives the decisive interpretation of John 4 for us, when the risen Jesus commissions the apostles

---

9. Carson, *John*, 216.

to be 'witnesses in Jerusalem and all Judea *and Samaria* and to the ends of the earth.' But John is already clearly pointing to that here, in the most striking way for any Jewish hearer. Yet, if they knew their Old Testament at all, they should have picked up on the fact that all along God made quite clear to Israel that he alone was the Saviour of all the ends of the earth (Isa. 45:22). He even recorded specific demonstrations of his mercy to individual Gentiles in the Scriptures to prove it! Think of the widow of Zarephath (1 Kings 17), or Naaman (2 Kings 5), and Jesus' words about them in Luke 4:24ff, to the fury of the Jews. These would be useful cross-references for the preacher here. The clear message is that the God of Israel apparently has wider horizons by far than the Israel of God.

But note: there is no room here for a false kind of sentimentalism. Jesus is *not* saying that the Samaritans were just as good as their Jewish neighbours. That is perhaps especially important for the Bible teacher to highlight in our day of relativism and tolerance. It is quite the opposite; he says plainly that their worship was *ignorant* worship (22). The mission of Jesus was specifically to the lost sheep of the house of Israel, for God's self revelation to Israel through all their history was alone the true revelation of the one true God. That is what makes it all the more remarkable, then, that his obedience to the Father on this occasion led him to Sychar's Well, and to a Samaritan, a religious mongrel.

To summarise thus far: if this story means anything, it spells out that Messiah Jesus is now crossing barriers into the pagan world. The journey is just beginning that will take his good news to the ends of the earth.

(2) Jesus came to save even the nobodies of this world

Jesus comes not only to a Samaritan, but specifically and intentionally to a woman. If to Israel the Samaritans were beyond the pale, so a woman in Israel was treated virtually as a religious nobody. Verse 27 is a telling aside in the narrative is it not? 'Just then his disciples returned and were surprised to find him talking with a woman but no-one asked, "What do you want", or, "Why are you talking with her?"' The rabbis of course would not teach the law to a woman since the rabbinic attitude was that women were inferior in every way. I think everyone knows the dreadful Jewish prayer, 'Blessed art thou O Lord who has not made me a woman'. We are naturally shocked by this, yet only a moment's thought suggests that this mindset is still going strong today in many non-Christian cultures. Recently a doctor in a hospital that deals with many immigrant families to Britain testified that his department now refuses to reveal any information from ultrasound scans of unborn babies concerning their sex. The implications of this are fairly horrific. If it is to be a girl, it may be unwanted and the road to abortion pursued.

It is unnecessary to spend time developing this point here, but it should be part of the preacher's task to draw out the meaning effectively, so as to show how striking is John's message about our Lord: that Messiah Jesus is here laying claim to be the Saviour even of women. He is their real liberator! So, for example, Mary Magdalene becomes the earliest recipient of the message that Jesus is risen (20:17), and Paul tells us in Romans 16 of Christian women who have worked so faithfully and effectively with him in the cause of the Gospel.

It does seem a pity that the preacher today cannot make this point, a truly glorious one, without having to deal with the confusion caused by a false Christian feminism. This wrong-headed kind of feminism seeks to obliterate all references to the natural order as taught by Paul in 1 Corinthians 11, or the church order taught clearly and unequivocally in the pastoral epistles. Each Christian teacher will therefore have to judge for himself, and handle this with wisdom according to the local situation. But here in John 4 the message is straightforward: Jesus is the saviour of all mankind, men and women, boys and girls. Because this is obvious to us, it is difficult to recreate the situation of John 4, but from verse 27 it is clear that the disciples are utterly amazed that Jesus is talking with a woman. Westcott has a very good comment here:

> A double question arose in the minds of the disciples. Could their master require a service from a woman? Or could he wish to commune with her as a teacher? Yet the disciples were content to wait. In due time he would remove their doubts. Even thus early they had learned to abide his time.[10]

This highlights and makes telling verse 27b as well as 27a. The disciples were astonished, but they had already learned that to be with Jesus meant to expect to be astonished! They would button their lips and look and learn. And what they were learning was that the good news of Jesus was not just for the religious somebodies like Nicodemus, but also for the irreligious nobodies like this woman.

(3) Jesus came to save even the morally degenerate of this world
This woman was a sinner. She was, by the nature of her life and behaviour, something that could only be condemned by

---

10. Westcott, *John*, 74

the law of God. Therefore from the religious point of view of a Jew she was an outsider with regard to her race, her sex and her way of life. Contact with such a spiritual leper could only defile the righteous. (Was that why she was on her own at the well in the heat of the day, instead of in the cool of the evening with the other women? The implication seems to be that even the corrupted Samaritan religion had ostracised her, let alone the 'pure' religion of Israel.)

Again, there is little need to enlarge on this point here, though we must not minimise the truth of the situation. This reality is so ruthlessly unearthed by the Lord in this conversation with the woman, and it is obviously an essential element in the story. As far as we, the readers, are concerned, we are forewarned and forearmed, for we know from John 3:17 that 'God did not send his Son into the world to condemn the world but to save the world through him'. What a commentary these great words are on the journey of Jesus to the well to meet a Samaritan sinner: He came not to condemn her but to save! Yet on the other hand, she must be made to confront her need and how faithfully Jesus revealed it to her (16-18); how faithfully he showed her desperate need for personal forgiveness and salvation. That is of course in part why her testimony reads as it does: 'He told me everything I ever did'. But see how gentle he is, even as he is faithful. Surely her words in verse 29 are doubly significant: not only does she marvel at his omniscience, and his pinpointing of her sin, but also – and even more important for her – that he should have known all about her and still treated her with courtesy, respect and dignity. To have known the worst about her, and still be so kind – this was the amazed awareness that convinced her that this must be the Messiah. Here is Grace and Truth at work!

The newspapers in our own day (of every hue) are so often like vultures circling around a kill, delighting to 'tell us everything' in exposing scandal and mercilessly placarding to the world every detail of the sordid lives of their victims. And how shameful and immoral the stories often are; how screwed up and broken the lives and relationships. So many are in such desperate need of a saviour! But then which of us does not? Who among us could stand alongside this woman and have our lives scrutinised and revealed in every detail by this Jesus, and not know our desperate need of salvation too? It should surely not be too hard for us to unfold this message in a telling way today.

Testimony leads to Illumination and true faith

The testimony of this woman, set in the whole context of the story before us, tells us plainly that Jesus has come on a mission to the idolatrous nations of the world, on a mission to the women of the world, and all the other downtrodden nobodies, and on a mission to all whom the law of God condemns as sinners. In short, this testimony leads to belief that here at Sychar's well is none other than the Saviour, the Saviour of mankind (42).

In this personal encounter with the woman, we have a striking example of the dawning illumination of the light of the gospel upon the mind and heart of a lost soul. For her it was the living Word of God in the flesh; the true light that lightens every human being was, in his encounter with her, shedding that light upon her, and forcing the distinction, exposing the conflict between light and darkness that is such a prominent theme for John throughout his Gospel. A struggle is taking place before our eyes, and she tries to evade with distraction (20) as people so commonly do. But as Jesus speaks with her we can see the dawn gradually brighten, until at last it bursts into the full break of day. At first she saw only a Jew (9); but shortly a prophet (19), then, in time, the Messiah (29) and at last, nothing less than the Saviour of the World (42). The light has shined in the darkness, and the darkness has not overcome it!

Life in the One Triune God

Testimony then leads to belief, now belief must lead to life. Recall that John 3:1-21 was Trinitarian through and through. What Nicodemus was offered was a knowledge of the true God, whom to know is life eternal. So it is here. Follow how this woman, ignorant just as Nicodemus was ignorant, was introduced to the good news of God.

First she was told about the living water, this gift from Christ which becomes in those who believe in him, a spring of water welling up to eternal life (10-14). (For the preacher the cross reference to John 7:37-9 will help to clarify and confirm this teaching.) John's Gospel is particularly rich in teaching on the Spirit of God. Here in John 4 it is the Spirit's work in slaking our spiritual thirst that is emphasised. It is clearly indicated that this woman, like many today, had tried to quench this thirst in other ways, including promiscuity. Remember God's words through Jeremiah:

> My people have committed two sins. They have forsaken me, the spring of living water, and have dug their own cisterns, broken cisterns that cannot hold water.
>
> Jer. 2:13

The applications of this to life today are legion, are they not? One important task for those of us preaching to people with little or no understanding of a biblical world view, and little or no vestige of a Christian moral framework, is that we must expose these dry and broken cisterns they have dug for themselves. There is demolition work to be done, showing up the false and feeble foundations people build their lives on. And we need to show that the reason why they are dry and broken, and ultimately do not satisfy, is that at root they have rejected the one and only true spring of living water, Christ himself.

It is worth noting that Jesus, in dealing with the syncretistic, religiously confused woman, does take a different route into his message from that with the thoroughly informed, religious man, Nicodemus. Nicodemus knew all about sin and guilt, about atonement and sacrifice, and Jesus' armour-piercing assault was on his religious pride. He was forcing Nicodemus to recognise his own impotence to remedy that sin before a holy God, who alone could cleanse the heart and give new birth. But here Jesus comes first to the woman's thirst, and touches the reality about the broken cisterns in her life, which she cannot deny. Only then does his rapier thrust force her to confront the fact that the very emptiness and failure to satisfy all stems from sinful behaviour, and ultimately from outright rejection of the one true God himself. We still find ourselves evangelising both these kinds of people today, too, and must be ready to use all the wisdom that Christ himself exhibited as we seek to 'demolish arguments and every pretension that sets itself up against the knowledge of God' in our own proclamation (2 Cor. 10:5).

Second, this woman is told about the Father, and how the Father seeks true worshippers. These will worship him neither on Mount Zion nor on Mount Gerizim, nor in any sacred place, but wherever they are in spirit and in truth, for

God is spirit (21-24). It is truly breathtaking that it is to this woman, and not even to a Nicodemus, that this revelation of the Father is given! That the Father should seek such as her, trapped as a Samaritan in a worship of falsehood, and as a woman trapped in a dishonourable way of life, is yet another bright gleam of free grace in the darkness of a fallen world.

But third, as we have seen already in studying this extraordinary encounter, she is confronted with the Son of Man. She meets in the flesh the eternal only-begotten of the Father, himself the very glory of the unseen God, full of grace and truth. And Jesus, in words pregnant with associations, declared at the end of this conversation these wonderful words, 'I who speak to you *am* he.' (26)

Eternal life, then, is the promise held out by Jesus to a Samaritan woman. And this is eternal life: that she might know the only true God and Jesus the Messiah whom God had sent to her (cf. 17:3).

Jesus: Saviour of the world

In both chapters 3 and 4, John the evangelist portrays to us Jesus the evangelist. The message of life is for a distinguished Jewish theologian (and theologians can still need evangelising today) and for a dishonourable Samaritan woman of no account (and such people should never be given up as beyond the possibility of being evangelised). In both chapters the elements of testimony, belief and life are strongly marked; indeed they are foundational to the structure of these two encounter stories. And in both chapters the divine mission is the salvation of mankind. Notice how often Jesus describes God as 'Him who sent me'. This is the work of God, and was for Jesus his very meat and drink (34). In both cases he is seen as the Saviour of the world, to which, in love, God sent him.

A wake-up call to the church

Naturally this is a powerful wake up call to the churches of
Christ today, as well as to individual Christians. It comes via
the words to the dim-witted disciples, in the call to harvest
(33-38). The scene is almost comical, and heavy with irony.
The woman's abandoned water pot stands testimony to her
wonderful discovery at last of the true and living water that
satisfies eternally, but the disciples can only think about food
to quell their hunger. Revival is virtually breaking out on the
road behind them, the villagers already coming in droves out
to the well to meet Jesus, while they care only about their
sandwiches! They seem totally unaware of the whole spiritual
drama, and can see only the mundane. How true to life it all
is, and how very contemporary!

The words of verse 35 are very forceful, 'Do you not say
four months more and then the harvest? I tell you open
your eyes and look at the fields, they are ripe for harvest.'
Leon Morris has culled two quotations which make apt
commentaries on these two halves.[11] First on verse 35a, 'four
months more and then the harvest', he quotes G Campbell
Morgan,

> If those disciples had been appointed a commission of
> inquiry as to the possibilities of Christian enterprise
> in Samaria, I know exactly the resolution they would
> have passed. The resolution would have been: "Samaria
> unquestionably needs our Master's message but it is not
> ready for it. There must first be ploughing, then sowing,
> and then waiting. It is needy, but it is not ready".

He then adds his own comment,

---

11. The Gospel according to John (Grand Rapids: Eerdmans, 1995),
247.

Can't you hear many of our ecclesiastical assemblies passing just such a motion? We are always ready to recognise needy areas but just as ready to find perfectly good reasons why we should do nothing for the present.

On verse 35b he quotes a description from H V Morton's geographical writing on Palestine:

As I sat by Jacob's Well a crowd of Arabs came along the road from the direction in which Jesus was looking, and I saw their white garments shining in the sun. Surely Jesus was speaking not of the earthly but of the heavenly harvest, and as he spoke I think it likely that he pointed along the road where the Samaritans in their white robes were assembling to hear his words.

So, chapter 4 is full of sending: the Father sends the Son (34), the Son sends the disciples (38), and we too are called and sent to harvest a crop for eternal life whether as sowers or reapers, or both. Let us conclude our study of this chapter with the final verses of the story.

Many of the Samaritans from that town believed in Jesus because of the woman's testimony, 'He told me everything I ever did'. So when the Samaritans came to him they urged him to stay with them and he stayed two days, and because of his words many more became believers. They said to the woman, 'We no longer believe just because of what you said, but now we have heard for ourselves and we know that this man really is the Saviour of the world.'

John 4:39-42

5

The Voice That Divides

What a great chapter this is! It is not so familiar, perhaps, as chapters 3 and 4, and therefore may be more demanding in preparation and preaching. We shall take the chapter as a whole and stay with the divisions and headings as printed in the NIV. The three sections are of very similar length; section one (1-15) records the third sign; section two (16-30) expounds the meaning of this sign, provoking yet more opposition and controversy, and section three (31-47) records the many testimonies to Jesus, despite which his opponents refused to believe.

The 'key' in John 5

As before, we make no attempt to offer a commentary on each and every verse, since the purpose is to enquire into John's method in setting out his material according to the pattern set out so explicitly in chapter 20:30-31. So far it has proved to be a remarkably exact description of the way John tells his stories of Jesus, and expounds his message, supporting the supposition that he uses this as a purposeful methodology, at least throughout the first half of his Gospel. That is not to say that all three of the elements (evidence, faith and life) appear with equal emphasis in each story or section of the Gospel; sometimes only two are prominent, and it may even be one strand that particularly stands out.

Here, sections one and two (the healing miracle and the exposition) both focus on John's great theme of life through the Son. Then in section three we have the fullest description yet of the many testimonies about Jesus that the Jews were given. Nevertheless, despite this, at the close of chapter 5 we find the plentiful evidence rejected, the whole thing summarised by the sad verse 40, 'Yet you refuse to come to me that you might have life.' The emphasis on the element of belief is here then, but it is here negatively, in terms of refusal to believe and have faith. It is worth saying that when Jesus describes refusal to believe in the face of the evidence, we get some of the most brilliant little cameos in the whole of the Gospel. Such snapshots of wilful unbelief are as true in principle today as ever, and they present powerful opportunity for the preacher to pass on the challenge that John presents us with from the pages of his book. So, we shall find that our old friends, testimony, belief and life control the entire chapter here in chapter 5.

1. The raising of a helpless man to new life (1-15)

One reason why this little story is often handled in a disappointing way is that the definitive interpretation of it, as given in section two, has not been sufficiently considered. For that reason it would be tempting to begin our discussion with section two. Suffice to say for the moment that in that section we are introduced to the twofold authority of the Son. First, he has authority to give life to whom he is pleased to give it (21), and this is perfectly exemplified in the third sign; second he has authority to judge all men for their condemnation (27). It is vital to see that these are not separable activities, for the gift of life is the sign and evidence that condemnation has been removed. The well-known verse 24 brings out this truth with great clarity:

> I tell you the truth, whoever hears my words and believes him who sent me, has eternal life and will not be condemned. He has crossed over from death to life.

So the cross-over from death to life is evidence that condemnation has been removed. With this in mind, let us go to the Sheep Gate and attend to what is going on there. We shall summarise just a few brief points here.

(1) Life comes through the word of Jesus

What we are witnessing at the pool called Bethesda is not dissimilar to the second sign at the end of the previous chapter. When the son of the royal official was healed, life was given to him by the powerful word of Jesus, and the same thing is happening here. It is given here in chapter 5 to whomsoever Jesus is pleased to give it. Nothing whatever points to any suggestion that the invalid of thirty-eight years is more worthy than the other crippled and helpless folk lying there. As far as we can see no faith is called for from him at all, unless it is the faith to obey the word of command, 'Get up, pick up your pallet and walk', and that is a response of faith that is thrust upon him in the very command itself.

What is abundantly clear here is that a creative act of power must take place if such a man, whose muscles and

sinews have long perished, could jump to his feet, gather up
his few belongings and be off without so much as a slip or a
stumble. This pathetic specimen has become in a moment a
man again. Jesus has called him from a pitiful, sub-human
existence into the ranks of humanity as it is meant to be.
Life has begun anew. Charles Wesley captures the thought
here perfectly:

> He speaks, and listening to his voice
> New life the dead receive.

(2) Forgiveness comes through the word of Jesus

It is noteworthy that the words that Jesus spoke to him are
exactly those spoken to the paralytic in Capernaum, recorded
in Mark 2:9. What a valuable clue this provides for us, for
the man at Capernaum was in need of forgiveness as well as
healing, and the healing was the outward and visible sign of
the invisible healing provided by the Lord Christ, a seal of
his God-given forgiveness.

It is worth interjecting here that although the 'harmonising'
approach to the Gospels has largely given way to one which
recognises the particular distinctives of the four Gospels
as works with their own characteristic aims and interests,
nevertheless we should not throw the baby out with the
bath-water and think there is no place for such comparisons
between the Gospels at all. Remember that underlying each
account is the actual historical activity of Jesus, and that we
are given the four Gospels side by side, bound together as
they are in our Bibles, not on their own, in vacuo. It is wholly
legitimate, and often crucial, when we are teaching to read
horizontally *across* these books, as well as vertically through
each one's own story. Indeed it is often by doing just this that
the particular distinctive emphasis of one writer becomes

clear in a certain context. So, taking the immediate context of our story and the context of John's Gospel seriously does not mean we must slavishly ignore the other Gospels, or indeed the rest of Scripture!

Here in Jerusalem, then, John portrays a very similar situation being enacted to the one which Mark records at Capernaum. If there were any doubt, it is made clear in stark fashion by verse 14, where Jesus finds him and says, 'See you are well, stop sinning or something worse may happen to you'. The plain implication is that he was not only paralytic but a sinner, and a very clear sinner in the sight of God. Of course the preacher will need to explain here that no rule is being laid down by this story that all sufferings are as a result of sins. (Carson, like other competent commentators, swiftly and succinctly unties the knots into which people get themselves tied on this subject; see pp 245-246 of his commentary). However, in this case a connection *is* clearly made between sin and suffering, and by Jesus himself.

(3) *Life and forgiveness are inseparable*

So, this third sign tells of the power of Christ to remove deserved condemnation and to grant life as a sign of that absolution. It is this reality, of course, that Paul expounds in his teaching on justification, where the verdict of no condemnation is always accompanied by union with Christ through the gift of the Spirit. Romans 6-8 is a classic exposition of this. We should ensure in our own teaching of the gospel that we never slip into the tendency to separate these inseparable things: either by majoring only on the new life in the Spirit, or indeed by focusing exclusively on the forensic side of justification alone. To do either is, to use Calvin's striking phrase, 'shamefully to rend Christ asunder'.

John's third sign, then, is a sign of salvation with all the richness this entails.

(4) *The Word that brings life always brings opposition*

Having witnessed life restored by the powerful word of Jesus, it is just worth a moment to absolve the healed man from the abuse that is customarily directed to him by commentators and preachers because of verse 15 'he went away and told the Jews it was Jesus who had made him well'. True, he may not have been made of the stuff of the hero in John 9, who dealt the Pharisees a few sharp uppercuts and then floored them completely with a knockout punch after his healing (9:25-34); that man was by any standard an outstanding character. But this poor man in chapter 5 does not deserve the doghouse. After all, he is not commanded not to tell who has healed him, as other characters are elsewhere. In fact, he plays a crucial role here in bringing the challenge of Jesus and his gospel into confrontation with the Jews who are determined to oppose and reject him. Hearing the voice of Jesus is, literally, the critical thing in this whole chapter. They too must hear his voice, and be judged by their chosen reaction to it; that is the point here.

Let us follow the sequence in verses 10-15. First the Jews rebuke the man for carrying his mat on the Sabbath. The man's reply (11) makes a lot of sense; he had been commanded to carry his mat by the very person who had power and authority to work so great a miracle on him. How could he do otherwise than do as his healer had said? Verse 12 suggests that his accusers had not witnessed the miracle themselves and therefore did not yet know who had performed it, and we are left hanging with tension in the air as to what is going to happen next. How are these cynics going to be dealt with? We are told that Jesus had slipped away without telling the healed man who he was (13). But when in the next verse we find that he purposely seeks the healed man out in private in order to warn him not to return to his old sinful ways (14), it already seems inevitable that his identity is going to be revealed to all: that he is going to come out into the open to confront both belief and unbelief. Verse 15 then simply records how this happens. After all, the man is bound to do all he can to defend himself from their very serious charge of Sabbath breaking, for he would almost certainly find himself in trouble otherwise. His point is simply that if the Jews want to question and condemn anyone, it should be the awesome person who had acted with God-like authority and power in releasing him from his bondage. That is precisely what they do (16), and it provokes the great discourse which follows in the next section.

2. The raising of all to life through the Son (16-30)

This is a wonderfully rich and full section and the preacher will be wise to work through it verse by verse with the help of the good commentators. However, a verse by verse lecture will not normally be the best kind of sermon or Bible talk. The task of the preacher must be to seize hold of the essentials of a section like this, so that his listeners do not lose the wood for the trees. The essentials here would seem to be two-fold: the person of Christ and the work of Christ.

The person of Christ

It is this that first confronts us in verses 16-18. To begin with the Jews are persecuting Jesus for what he does on the Sabbath. It is perfectly clear here (and elsewhere) that

Jesus deliberately and provocatively worked miracles on the Sabbath. When he explains why he must work on the Sabbath in the breathtaking words of verse 17, the charge against him becomes the far more serious one of making himself equal with God. From here, the logic of the Lord's words leads inexorably to the magnificent climax 'That all may honour the Son just as they honour the Father. He who does not honour the Son does not honour the Father, who sent him' (23). John is determined that the person of Jesus should be fully explored in chapter after chapter of the Gospel, and so it is here in chapter 5.

The work of Christ

The second essential in this section of teaching concerns the work of Christ. This follows logically; it is because of who he is, that he does what he does. He is equal with God, for 'the Word was God' (1:1), yet as the God-man subordinate to the Father. He must do what the Father does, but do it here in the world, the world to which the Father has sent him. Let us put it in its simplest way, even though the reality is infinitely profound and beyond our little minds. First, his work is to give life, often described here as raising people from the dead, whether spiritually or physically. Secondly, his work is to exercise judgment over all men.

This work is spelt out in verses 19-23. Notice again that there are not here two separable activities. As verse 24 made especially clear, when life is bestowed, this is itself a sufficient sign that condemnation has been removed and therefore the believer has passed from death (the wages of sin) to life (the gift of God).

Following this, the application is made in verses 24-27 to the present, and in verses 28-30 to the future. The key verse to the first little section is verse 25,

> I tell you the truth, a time is coming and has now come
> when the dead (that is the spiritually dead) will *hear the*
> *voice* of the Son of God, and those who hear will *live*.

The key verse in the second little section of application is
verse 28-29,

> Do not be amazed at this, for a time is coming when all
> who are in their graves (the physically dead) will *hear*
> *his voice* and come out. Those who have done good will
> *rise to live* and those who have done evil will *rise to be*
> *condemned*.

It is well worth noting that the verb *rise* here in verse 29 is
exactly that used by Jesus in commanding the cripple to 'get
up', in verse 9. (It is a pity that the NIV often misses John's
deliberate repeated usage of the same word to drive home
a point by opting for variety in its translation). Here he is
making a clear and definite link that he means us to notice
between hearing, rising, and living: 'Rise!' (9), 'hear and live
[now]' (25) and 'rise to live [then]' (29)

In summary: life from the dead in our spiritual experience
now, and life from the dead in the future, fuller and final
experience on the resurrection day at Christ's coming, is the
focus of this passage. This is the gift of God, and it comes
only through hearing the life-giving voice of God himself
in Jesus. The word that imparts spiritual life now, promises
eternal life then. It is *assured*: 'he has crossed over'; it is also
urgent: the time for hearing 'has now come'.

Thinking about the sermons
Having made an effort here to seize the essentials in this
second section, are you persuaded that there is too much here
for one sermon? It could be taken in one – indeed the whole
chapter could be taken in one – but that would mean very

definitely selecting essentials, even if you had an extended time for developing the exposition. But this section would make a grand four-week series using precisely the paragraphs the NIV sets out for us (so perhaps redeeming the deficiency above!)

Let us take the space here to plan a possible series like that, with titles that will accurately describe what is going to be taught, and will also perhaps draw people in to listen. We should not be obsessed by having clever titles, since the actual preaching is far, far more important. It can become quite counter-productive. But it can be a good exercise if it helps to pinpoint the meaning of each section, and thereby discover the potential for reaching the minds and hearts of our hearers. So, if you are going to strive for titles, try to use analytical ones that serve your preaching, and use them to give the sermon focus. Here is one attempt; no doubt you will be able to do better! The sermon card or the notice board (or web site!) might read with a main title: 'Father and Son' or perhaps, 'Like Father, Like Son'.

Like Father, Like Son
The amazing truth about Jesus –
an explanation of John chapter 5:16-30

1. No rest on Sundays! (16-18)
This will help to show that God does not rest on the Sabbath Day, otherwise the universe would collapse.

2. What Jesus is doing today and tomorrow (19-23)
This helpfully moves the focus from what he did on the cross and by the resurrection on to today and tomorrow: he is in fact giving life to people *today* and condemning people *today*, who do not receive his gospel of salvation.

3. Have you ever heard God's voice? (24-27)
Because the answer to that question is that if you have
heard his voice you will be alive, and if you have not you
stand condemned already.

4. When the graves are opened (28-30)
The focus on the absolute certainty of our mortality, and
facing up to the judgment all will inevitably meet.

So, there are four possible sermon suggestions on this
section, verses 16-30. By dividing it up like this you have
the opportunity to give proper development to each of these
crucial points, and also to ensure that you keep the central
theme of the urgency of the message about hearing the voice of
the Son of God right before your hearers for four consecutive
weeks. If you were preaching through a longer section of the
Gospel, you could probably afford to take larger sections for
each sermon, because many of the themes are recurring. But it
is often a useful approach even then to slow down from time
to time and focus on one smaller portion for several weeks,
and let people really dwell on the message. You could equally
make it a longer series: the above four preceded by one on
the first section (1-15), which would allow you to major on
the miracle story itself, perhaps focusing on forgiveness and
life, and drawing some initial key links to the exposition that
follows; then continuing on with a further series of messages
on the final section (31-47). To this section we now turn.

3. Testimonies about Jesus (31-47)
This section (31-47) is by far the richest on the whole theme
of testimony so far. Why does it appear just here? The reason
lies before us in the situation described in the chapter as a
whole, for it is now that the bitter controversy with the Jewish
religious establishment begins in earnest. The Lord Jesus has

come out into the open by the unmistakable claims for deity he makes for himself in verses 17 and 22-23. These claims cannot be misunderstood and the Jews do not misunderstand them. But far from respecting what Jesus says or responding in belief from this day onwards, they try harder than ever to encompass his destruction (18).

A hostile jury

Such a furious reaction on the part of the Jews is, on the face of it, not very surprising. Put yourself in the shoes of one of the Jews who was present that day, and listen to Jesus testifying about himself in the seemingly blasphemous way. It is doubtful whether you would have thought any differently than your fellow religionists. Even a miracle would hardly affect your judgment. To take a ridiculously small analogy: an invitation to a top London hotel is received to hear a man who can only be regarded as a notorious phoney on the healing circuit. The letter is richly embossed in gold, and couched in the most extreme language, both concerning the spiritual power and authority of the healer himself and the talk he will give, and the benefits of transformed ministry certainly to be received by attending. Now if perchance one of the miracle cures that this man claims to have worked is actually wholly substantiated would one even then give this invitation a second thought? Almost certainly not! Incidentally, it is interesting that the literature this man sent did not contain one single testimony to the spiritual standing of the healer himself from a reputable church leader in this country. Would no-one in this country vouch for him except himself and his fancy literature?

This does seem to throw some light on a verse like 31, 'If I testify about myself my testimony is not valid.' If Jesus arrived on the scene from nowhere and testified to himself, however eloquently and fervently, such testimony would inevitably be suspect as to its validity. Thus if the testimony of Jesus to himself stood alone, and was in a sense the whole story, it might be difficult to find fault with the Jewish leaders and their refusal to accept his word for it all. But of course the testimony to Jesus given by himself as here in section two is *not* the whole story! The appearance of the Lord was not a sudden bolt from the blue without any antecedents. The whole story of human history, no less, had been preparing for it, and that preparation had been focused in the most extraordinary way upon one exclusive people, the Jews. It was their own prophets and preachers who had long prepared the way of the Lord; their sacred scriptures themselves had at their very heart testimony about the coming One. Throughout his narrative, John has already shown how clearly the Old Testament speaks of Jesus (see, for example, 1:45, 2:22, 3:10 and 45-46 here in this chapter). So no, there is no excuse. The testimony comes from every direction, and cannot be avoided.

This, then, is the raison d'être of this section. Testimony to Jesus does not depend on his word alone, though of course he is entirely trustworthy when he does testify on his own behalf (8:14). There are others who testify concerning him, and whose testimonies Jesus now sets before his opponents in this third section. First, the testimony of John the Baptist (33), second, the testimony of the works: the signs and the miracles (36), third, the testimony of the Father (37), and finally the testimony of the Scriptures (39), including the reference to Moses in verse 46.

Putting the text in context
Now pause for a moment; just a caution is necessary. In our desire to be relevant as preachers we can too easily collapse the

past into the present, and in this case jump straight to urging our listeners to consider for themselves the claims that these testimonies make upon us today. Indisputably there is some real force in this: the Old Testament Scriptures, for example, do testify to us of Christ and should be read accordingly. However, section three must be read first in its historical setting, for the fact is that Jesus was talking to specific people, the Jews of his own day, and we must recognise this. We must deal with this (and every) passage of Scripture in its literary and historical context, not as a piece of flotsam which appears before us in a haphazard or chance fashion.

Sometimes people fear that when we make this point we are saying that individual verses of Scripture, which may have been very precious verses to them, become somehow devalued. But that is far from the case. Indeed it is quite the opposite; putting the texts in their proper context never detracts from their meaning, but only fills the truth fuller than it was before.

Take, for example, the famous words 'Let not your hearts be troubled. Believe in God, believe also in me' (John 14:1) which are so often read at funerals, and are in themselves words of great comfort to the believer. We hear the kindly and wonderful voice of our Saviour, and are rightly comforted. But, if we go to the context, we find that there is much more here than this. We find that the immediate context is that of the disciples' misunderstanding and weakness, and particularly Peter's betrayal (13:18ff, 36-38). So it is even in the face of this human sin and extreme failure that Jesus does not rebuke, but gives this assurance of peace. And further, we find that this assurance rests on the work that Jesus is about to accomplish through his death and resurrection. He is going to prepare a place for his followers not after his death, but actually *through* his atoning death (14:2); if that can be accomplished, then they can have absolute peace that this promise of his coming again to bring them to heaven is assured (3). Hence the priority message of the risen Jesus for the disciples that he is returning to heaven having accomplished all this (20:17); in other words their hope *is* secure because of the resurrection of Jesus from the dead! Now, having seen this, how much *more* full are these words 'Let not your hearts be troubled' for us today as post-resurrection believers, who have that sure knowledge of Christ's completed work! Have these good and comfortable words of Jesus not been given the full richness and wonder they deserve?

So here, it is in the context of whom Jesus was addressing that the force of these testimonies, if we may put it like this, increases tenfold. We cannot go into each in detail, but in order to make this point we shall give brief attention to each of the witnesses.

Truly Damning Testimony
(1) *The testimony of John the Baptist*
Think of the testimony of the Baptist (33-35), and notice what is said. The Jews had in fact taken John's ministry very seriously indeed and sent deputations to inquire of him (1:19 ff.). For a time, they had chosen to enjoy his light (35). Compare Mark's reference to this, when he tells us that the whole population of Judea and Jerusalem went out to John to be baptised by him in the wilderness, confessing their sins (Mark 1:5).

Yes, the testimony of John had been very powerful: it had prepared the way of the Lord; his voice had echoed throughout the land, and no-one could deny the

overwhelming effect of the forerunner's ministry. Had he
not testified to all that Jesus was the Son of God, the Lamb
of God, the baptiser with the Holy Spirit? Indeed he had, in
his role as the greatest prophet of them all, and no Jew of any
sincerity could now easily dismiss such testimony as of little
significance. In the light of that, look again at verses 33-35
and sense the force of it:

> You have sent to John and he has testified to the truth.
> [34] Not that I accept human testimony; but I mention it
> that you may be saved. [Notice the positive note there:
> Jesus refers to John not to score a point, but to remind
> them of the message of salvation] [35] John was a lamp
> that burned and gave light, and you chose for a time to
> enjoy his light.

Do you see that this reference must have its first application
to the people of his day rather than to us? It was actually a
damning indictment of their fickle and empty repentance
and outright rejection of the gospel.

(2) *The testimony of the signs*
Think of the testimony of the works Jesus was doing (36).

> I have testimony weightier than that of John. For the very
> work that the Father has given me to finish, and which I
> am doing, testifies that the Father has sent me.

While it is true that these words still testify to Jesus today,
consider the impact of them on contemporary opponents
of Jesus, who simply could not deny what they had seen.
John 11:47 ff. is the classic example of this. The Jews continue
to refuse to believe in the face of indisputable miracles such
as the raising of Lazarus. This was not done in a corner. The
point that Jesus is making in this section is that the Jews of

his day are absolutely without excuse. They could not deny the greatness of John and his ministry, nor could they deny the greatness of Jesus' works. Yet they simply refused to let such powerful witness affect them. It just shows that if we do not want to believe, nothing will convince us.

(3) *The testimony of the Old Testament*
Consider the testimony of the Scriptures themselves (39), so precious to the pious Jews of Jesus' day.

> You diligently study the Scriptures because you think by them you possess eternal life. These are the Scriptures that testify about me.

Yes, the Jewish opponents of Jesus did indeed search the Scriptures. Westcott[12] comments that the original word here for search actually describes that minute and intense investigation of Scripture which issued in the allegorical and mystical interpretations of the Mishnah. He quotes Rabbi Hillel as saying, 'He who has gotten to himself words of Torah, has gotten himself life of the world to come.' Here was a superstitious attitude to the outward letter of the Law, that can rightly be called bibliolatry, and in all this they miss the divine purpose of the Scriptures, which was to testify to Jesus. Acts 10:43 is a useful cross-reference on the theme of the prophetic testimony to Jesus, and Romans 9:4-5 tells of the vast spiritual privileges that Israel enjoyed and which for so many were in vain.

Why could they not understand that Word of God? Because, in an illuminating phrase, 'God's word did not dwell in them' (37). Does this not explain, for instance, why the Scriptures can be minutely studied by rationalistic

---

12. Westcott, *John*, 91.

scholarship, or by sectarian interpreters, yet not lead to faith in Jesus, the unique Son of God. Why? Because God's word does not dwell in their hearts.

(4) *The testimony of God the Father himself*

The final witness is the testimony of the Father himself (32, 37). The commentators differ as to the precise meaning of this testimony and so dogmatism would be unwise. There could be references to the drama of his baptism, though John does not draw attention to the voice in his own account of this (1:32). But could verses 37-38 contain a possible key?

> And the Father who has sent me has himself testified concerning me. You have never heard his voice nor seen his form, nor does his word dwell in you, for you do not believe the one he sent.

You have never heard God's voice nor seen his *form* says Jesus, something which the Jews themselves would of course insist on too. But note the explanation '*because* you do not believe the one he sent.' It is a constant refrain in this chapter, and throughout John, that Jesus is the one the Father has sent to them. And this Son whom the Father has sent repeatedly says that he *speaks* only the words that the Father has given him to speak and he *does* only what his Father does. So, in hearing Jesus they were hearing the Father and in seeing Jesus they were seeing the Father. This perfect obedience to the Father by the Son secures for us in Jesus a sufficient revelation of the Father—for those who *will* see, through faith. The form of God the Father *is* Jesus.

This is Paul's subject in the great Christ hymn in Philippians 2, where the staggering message is that Jesus *is* the form of God – the very image and glory of the eternal God. Yet his image is made known to man by taking on himself the form of a servant, and humbling himself all the way to death, even to death on a cross. But this is just what the Jews *would not see.* This is a God they did not want, and would not have. That was the fatal stumbling block, the scandal they could not stomach (1 Cor 1:23).

Summing up the evidence

What then does Jesus uniquely reveal to us of his Father? What is the unique collective testimony of these witnesses? We need look no further than one example, verses 22-23, where we are told the Father has entrusted all judgment to the Son. This is one aspect of the Father's own testimony to the Son. What the Father testifies is this: that he, Jesus, the man in front of the Jews that day, and he alone, is fitted to be the sole judge of all things and of all men, both now and at the end of the age. What a testimony! It is beyond human imagination. Yet so it is. To adapt an old prayer, it is to Jesus at God's right hand that all human hearts are open, and all desires known, and from whom no secrets are or can be hidden.

The verdict: light wholeheartedly rejected

The force of verses 31-40 therefore is extremely clear. The opponents of Jesus are inexcusable in their rejection of him. They could hardly complain of being kept in the dark. Illumination in plenty had been given to guide their steps to Jesus. Who could forget that burning and shining light in the desert, John the Baptist? Who could deny the reality of the unique words and works of Jesus? And daily they searched the Scriptures which testified then (as now) to Jesus. All this raises the question, of course, of why did they not believe?

His own did not receive him

So we come to the final paragraph and the problem par excellence before our author, and later the apostle Paul, the problem of Israel's unbelief. We must leave you to the commentaries here for a full discussion of these final verses of the chapter. Carson is particularly helpful. But for preaching it would probably pay dividends to make much of the penetrating question of verse 44. The defendant, who has been the subject of the four witnesses in the preceding verses, now turns prosecutor and judge, and Jesus' words are a rapier thrust to the heart. Read 41-47 to yourself with an emphasis on verse 44.

> How can you believe if you accept praise from one an-
> other, yet make no effort to obtain the praise that comes
> from the only God?

By contrast Jesus does not look on man's praise and approbation (41). If he had done so he would have sought to be a very different kind of Messiah than the one he was. He would have been a king that the Jews could accept and welcome. It is still true that religious pretenders who come in their own name and for their own glory seldom fail to find a willing audience among formal and nominal believers. Few such come offering the scandal of a cross to carry. That was what Jesus offered, and it was a deeply offensive stab at the heart of the pride and dignity of his Jewish contemporaries. So it is today.

The voice that still divides

When this same gospel is faithfully opened up and proclaimed today to our own contemporaries, whether religious or ir-religious, we shall find the same reactions, because the heart of man has not changed with time. At root we are all the same. But praise be to God that he is indeed still at work today, calling men and women to rise up and live through the same voice of the Son, breathed out in power by the Spirit from the Scriptures. But those who through the preaching of the Scriptures today do hear the message that the Jews of Jesus' day heard, and reject as they did the voice of Jesus calling them to choose life, they too shall stand accused and condemned by these same witnesses.

This ought to add a solemnity and great burden to our task in preaching. Every time the message of the gospel is proclaimed, every time one of these witnesses in Scripture gives testimony to him through our preaching, be it John the Baptist in the Gospels or Moses in the Pentateuch, men and women are either coming closer to the light, or else – terrible thought – adding to the accusation against themselves on the day of Judgment. Moreover, the contemporary challenge of verse 44 is a powerful one for every pastor and preacher, every scholar, theologian and writer, every church leader or person of influence in the churches. Whose praise are we seeking? Whose acceptance must we have? Whom do we seek to please in all things? Let us remember Paul's words, 'If I was still trying to please men I would not be a servant of Christ' (Gal 1:10) – and take heed how we ourselves hear.

6

The Lord of Life

Coming to the long and fascinating chapter 6 we stick to the task of investigating John's evangelistic method. We shall have no space to digress on controversial matters such as, for example, the relationship of this chapter to the Lord's Supper. Much more important for the Bible teacher is to establish how John saw fit to proclaim the evangel himself, since in the end this must greatly influence our own gospel preaching today.

The chapter before us can reasonably fall into three major sections, at least from the point of view of the teacher. The first (1-24) comprises the two great miracles: the feeding of the five thousand, and the walking on the water. The feeding miracle clearly seems to control the whole chapter. The second major section (25-59) is made up of our Lord's teaching on the bread of life. This is a divinely given interpretation on the feeding of the five thousand; John the apostolic preacher, guided uniquely by the Spirit, links what was taught in the

Capernaum synagogue (59) with what happened on the mountainside (3). The third section (60-71), which we shall only touch on, concentrates on the division between professing disciples, which leads to the departure of many, so leaving behind just the twelve, including the betrayer-to-be, Judas.

At first glance it might be tempting to make too neat a system: to say section one is basically testimony (which indeed it is), section two basically on life, (which is expounded here more fully than hitherto), and section three on belief and unbelief, a contrast we are becoming accustomed to in John's Gospel. But we do not want to impose a rigid pattern on the text, despite the fact that in some places the text segments do indeed seem to fall conveniently into these thematic divisions. It is better to recognise that here in this chapter all three fundamental elements in John's presentation of the Gospel emerge in all the three sections, in other words, throughout the chapter. Take, for example, testimony. Section one is John's testimony to Jesus as he recounts these two mighty supernatural acts. In section two we find Jesus' own testimony to himself, and section three includes the testimony of Peter and of the twelve to their Lord and Master. So to that extent all three sections contain testimony and witness. When we come to belief and life we find them as the warp and weft of section two and in a measure in section three. This mingling of his key themes is very characteristic of John as we shall find especially in section two. An excellent description of John's method is found in Robert Law's commentary on the first epistle of John, when he writes about the style and structure of that letter. It is very relevant to the Gospel too.

> The word that, to my mind, might best describe St. John's
> mode of thinking and writing in this Epistle is *spiral*. The

course of thought does not move from point to point in a straight line. It is like a winding staircase always revolving around the same centre, always recurring to the same topics, but at a higher level. Or, to borrow a term from music, one might describe the method as contrapuntal. The Epistle works with a comparatively small number of themes, which are introduced many times, and are brought into every possible relation to one another.[13]

If the leading themes of 1 John are righteousness, love and belief, in John's Gospel they are witness (testimony), belief and life.

Jesus The Lord Of Nature

We begin with section one (1-24), where in fact there is nothing spiral or contrapuntal, just straightforward reporting of John's testimony to Jesus. We shall be limited to three brief statements about this section and these stories.

(1) Testimony to a unique creative power

These two stories are of unique miraculous power, demonstrated in ways seen neither before nor since in their sheer magnitude. The miserable attempts to rationalise the miracles of the feeding of the five thousand and the walking on the water are familiar to all theological students, and also to many ordinary Christians (perhaps particularly of former generations) who have read William Barclay's popular daily Bible reading notes. A scholar of his worth and standing explained them away, and by so doing simply popularised what liberal scholars had been teaching for many years. It is

---

13. Robert Law, *The Tests of Life, a Study of the First Epistle of St. John* [3rd Ed.] (Edinburgh T & T Clark, 1913). Available online at www.dabar.org/NTCommentaries.htm.

hard to conceive that anyone really found such alternative explanations even remotely plausible, but there can be no doubt of the harm they did to generations of church-going people. Yet to dispute the record here not only deprives the Word made flesh of his glory, but leaves the reputation of the Gospel writers as honest and competent chroniclers in tatters.

One man who came through a youthful period of scepticism was Archbishop William Temple, who in his later writing on John's Gospel, would write as follows on the feeding of the five thousand (quoted in Leon Morris' commentary):

> It is clear that every evangelist supposed our Lord to have wrought a creative act and for myself I have no doubt that this is what occurred. This however is credible only if St John is right in his doctrine of our Lord's person. If the Lord was indeed God Incarnate the story presents no insuperable difficulties but of course such a creative act is quite incredible if he is other or less than God Incarnate.[14]

Precisely. This leads on to the second statement.

(2) *Testimony to a unique divine identity*

These stories are, without question, stories of God at work among men. God is the Creator, God is the ruler of the great deep, and here is God Incarnate in just such activities. He, who was the agent of creation (John 1:3), feeds an immense and hungry crowd with five small barley loaves, (don't you love the 'small' there?) and two small fish (9). But he doesn't just satiate the vast crowd from this little healthy eating, low calorie packed lunch; No! – the leftovers required twelve big

---

14. Morris, *John*, 300.

baskets to take them away home! (The 'share and share alike' theories of explaining away the miracle, that everyone was shamed into bringing out their own sandwiches by the young boy's actions, never seemed to take this troublesome fact into account.) Similarly, he who rules the raging of the sea walks serenely through the storm to his beleaguered disciples and brings them safely to the haven where they longed to be.

Remember the context. All this is taking place among a people steeped in the Old Testament Scriptures, full of the knowledge of the one, true, omnipotent, creator God, the LORD, the God of Israel, before whom nations fall, and at whose feet even the very wonders of nature bow in reverent praise. John is also writing primarily for those who would cotton on pretty quickly to the kind of allusions to deity he is clearly making here in his testimony to Jesus. Obvious cross-references in the Old Testament include Psalm 65 and Psalm 107, where it becomes crystal clear even to us that John is claiming for Jesus identity with this unique and only God:

> You [The LORD] answer us with awesome deeds of right-eousness, O God our Saviour, the hope of all the ends of the earth and of the farthest seas, [6] who formed the mountains by your power, having armed yourself with strength, [7] who stilled the roaring of the seas, the roaring of their waves, and the turmoil of the nations.
>
> Psalm 65:5-8

> [Some] went out on the sea in ships; they were merchants on the mighty waters. [24] They saw the works of the LORD, his wonderful deeds in the deep. [25] For he spoke and stirred up a tempest that lifted high the waves. [26] They mounted up to the heavens and went down to the depths; in their peril their courage melted away. [27] They reeled and staggered like drunken men; they were at their wits' end.

[28] Then they cried out to the LORD in their trouble, and he brought them out of their distress. [29] He stilled the storm to a whisper; the waves of the sea were hushed. [30] They were glad when it grew calm, and he guided them to their desired haven. [31] Let them give thanks to the LORD for his unfailing love and his wonderful deeds for men.

Psalm 107:23-31

Even C H Dodd, who was really a liberal, can say of the words *ego eimi (I am)* in verse 20 that it seems more than probable that it is to be understood here, as elsewhere, as the equivalent of the divine name. Here, then, is John's testimony to a unique divine identity, God himself at work in the world of men.

(3) *Testimony to a new world order*

These stories are also stories that bear witness to a new creation and new created order. All through his Gospel John has a consistent message for us of a new world order that is coming, and indeed is breaking in already in the person of Jesus himself. There is water into wine in chapter 2, a new birth for a master in Israel in chapter 3, a new way of worship for the Samaritans in chapter 4, and a new 'time' coming, repeated constantly (4:21-23 and 5:25-28). Throughout these chapters John is spelling out the nature of the new world which is being brought into being by its creator and Lord, and the clear testimony here is that the creator and Lord is none other than this Jesus.

In summary, these two marvellous stories, these two marvellous miracles, are John's significant witness to Jesus. Jesus as the bread of life, the heavenly food of his people, sustaining and satisfying them in the wilderness of this world, is for most Christians a familiar idea. Perhaps less frequently considered is Jesus as the controller of the seas. The Hebrews, as you probably know, feared the sea as personifying the chaos of the massed powers that stood in opposition against God. Hence the expressions in, for example, Psalm 46:2-3. (In this regard it is worth comparing Mark 4:39 with Mark 1:25; see how Jesus speaks to the waves as he speaks to the demons.)

Divine mastery over the sea is frequently dwelt on in Scripture. Think of the Exodus story for example. Thus what we are seeing here in John's Gospel is that even the treacherous floods cannot prevent God's people reaching the destination that he has for them. And of course in the new world there will be 'no more sea'; it will have disappeared, cast out of the new heavens and earth and taking with it all who have set themselves eternally against God and his people (Rev. 21:1). You can find lots of references to this in any good Bible dictionary under the titles of sea, storm, water etc. and it is probably worth drawing attention to this point about the associations of the sea imagery here in the exposition. It not only sheds a great deal of light on the significance of this story, but also just drops a little hermeneutical key into the minds of your hearers that will help them when they come across other similar imagery elsewhere, such as in the Psalms quoted above (not to mention giving reassurance to the sailors and surfers of this world who might otherwise find the prophecy of a heaven only for landlubbers quite appalling!)

We should by now have seen enough from this brief discussion of section one to see clearly the thrust of John's witness to Jesus as the Son of God, the Creator, the Lord of nature.

Jesus the Bread of Life

A section like verses 25-59 certainly needs a great deal of hard labour from the preacher in his study before he dares enter his pulpit and teach it. Fortunately for preachers there are now many superb helps through the labours of reliable scholars, and we must not shirk from using them. It is also worth adding that we ought not to allow our reading of commentaries to be too narrow, as though only those who are sound through and through (in our own view) can have anything to teach us. Often, in fact, it is in reading those whom one may disagree with profoundly at points, that some of the most fruitful lines of enquiry are suggested, and the most imaginative insights found for the preacher. We need to learn to read discriminatingly, of course, but that will not happen unless we do read widely.

But our job here is not that of the commentator, but to demonstrate John's method in this discourse in order to help us teach John's message effectively ourselves. His method is rarely clearer than in these verses where once again the familiar themes of testimony, faith and life reappear. To adapt Robert Law's words quoted earlier on, this discourse works with a comparatively small number of themes which are introduced many times and are brought into every possible relationship to one another. Theme one is testimony; here in this section it is the Lord's own witness to himself. Theme two is life, the life Jesus brings to the world (33). Theme three is belief: that is, the true nature of saving faith. These are our familiar friends, testimony, belief and life, and a reading of this section will show these three brought into close connection and interdependence.

One way in which the preacher might handle this rich material is by a series of three sermons. To do this it is essential to identify the central thrust of each theme as it is presented by John, which is usually easily recognised by its constant repetition. Here we can only draw attention to major seams, which appear very clearly; but as you work it out in the study no doubt you will be able to dig out and display the full riches from these seams yourself.

(1) Where did Jesus come from?
The first theme is Jesus' testimony about himself. *Where did Jesus come from?* would be a useful title, with a starting point at verses 41-42.

> At this the Jews began to grumble about him because he said, "I am the bread that came down from heaven." They said, "Is this not Jesus, the son of Joseph, whose father and mother we know? How can he now say, 'I came down from heaven'?

Here is an astonishing contrast. The Jewish listeners think they know where Jesus comes from: he is the son of Joseph. But Jesus is at pains to tell them where he really comes from, since he is the Son of God. Repeatedly Jesus is saying 'I came down from heaven' (33, 38, 51). Note similarly the repeated references to the bread from heaven, for example verses 31, 32, 50 and 58. According to his own testimony, Jesus has come from God. But of course it is not sufficient to affirm this without making absolutely clear what is being claimed. After all, according to John 1:6, 'There came a man who was sent from God whose name was John.' Was Jesus then to be another great prophet like the Baptist? Nicodemus had gone as far as introducing himself with these words, 'Rabbi we know you are a teacher who has come from God' (3:2). Was Jesus then just another brilliant and God-given teacher for Israel? Not at all. What Jesus does in this synagogue sermon is to claim for himself in a host of ways a quite unique relationship to God the Father, whose Son he is: a relationship that differentiates him from all others who have gone before.

We do not have space to go into all these wonderful sayings here, but an exposition that clearly presented four or five of these statements and their significance would leave people with no doubt that Jesus had a unique relationship with the Father: a relationship not shared with any other prophet or teacher that Israel had known, or indeed that the world has known ever since.

> It is written in the Prophets: 'they will all be taught by God.' Everyone who listens to the Father and learns from him comes to me. No-one has seen the Father except the one who is from God; only he has seen the Father.
>
> John 6:45-46

Unique claims are always explosive!
Obviously developing the implication of this claim would bring one easily from the biblical world of first century Israel into the contemporary world of today, with all its religious traditions, gurus, spirit guides, philosophies and the rest. It would bring one inevitably into a head-on collision with the prevailing pluralism of our western world, with the absolute claim of the uniqueness, the superiority and the supremacy of Christ over all other pretenders, and their claims, and their followers. Make no mistake, this message is as much dynamite among the 'tolerant' post-modern today as it was among the Jewish intolerant of Jesus' day!

And it was dynamite in Jesus' day. What we seem to have here in chapter 6 is an outworking of 5:17-18, when Jesus said to the Jews, 'My Father is always at his work to this very day, and wI, too, am working.' We are clearly told that because of this 'the Jews tried all the harder to kill him' for 'he was even calling God his own Father, making himself equal with God.' But, for those who will accept it, here in John 6 is the evidence of that perfect and unique unity between the Father and the Son.

> All that the Father gives me will come to me, and whoever comes to me I will never drive away. [38] For I have come down from heaven not to do my will but to do the will of him who sent me. [39] And this is the will of him who sent me, that I shall lose none of all that he has given me, but raise them up at the last day. [40] For my Father's will is that everyone who looks to the Son and believes in him shall have eternal life, and I will raise him up at the last day.
>
> John 6:37-40

Space forbids the development of this great theme, but what is now becoming apparent is that when John tells us of Jesus' testimony to himself he is at the very same time telling us of Jesus' testimony to his Father. This is consistently John's method for proclaiming the Father: he proclaims the Son. For he who has seen the Son has seen the Father who sent him (cf. John 14:9-11); conversely, he who has not accepted the Son, or who will not accept the uniqueness of the Son's revelation of God, has not seen and cannot see, the one, true and living God. It is as stark as that, and just as offensive today.

(2) *This is the Life!*

'I am the bread of life', the first of the great 'I ams', repeated in verses 35, 48 and 51, is the great focus of the second theme here: life. As always in John's Gospel life is presented as something the believer experiences now, in this age, and as something the believer will experience in the age to come. There is no one-sided emphasis here. Some commentators speak as though realised eschatology is all you get in John's Gospel, but here in this chapter repeatedly we are given that glorious and comforting promise, 'I will raise him up at the last day' (39, 40, 44, 54), and are told that he who eats of this bread will 'live forever' (51, 58). Yet neither is there anything of an under-realised eschatology, an emphasis on the life to come to the exclusion of the life we can find in all its fullness here and now in this world through Christ. Every true believer knows in experience eternal life begins here and now: 'I tell you the truth he who believes *has* everlasting life' (47); 'Whoever eats my flesh and drinks my blood *has* eternal life' (54). And of course there is above all the lovely assurance of verse 51, a promise of satisfaction and fulfilment now that the world, with all its promises and with all its hopes, simply cannot provide.

> I am the bread of life. He who comes to me will never go
> hungry and he who believes in me will never be thirsty.

Sermon two, then, would go out of its way to present this understanding of eternal life as the knowledge of the only true God and of his Son Jesus Christ, both here and now (17:3), and that fuller knowledge that will be ours at the resurrection. The aim would be to draw out these two strands from Jesus' teaching in this passage, establishing as clearly as possible from his own words the emphasis on the life now, and the life still to come, neither downplaying the one or the other. But it would be helpful, and probably essential, to show how this great theme of the 'now' and the 'not yet' pervades the teaching of the New Testament, albeit briefly. This will help not only to clarify in the listener's mind the doctrine, but also to reinforce confidence in the trustworthiness and consistency of Scripture. A useful cross-reference would be Paul's great words in 1 Cor. 13:12:

> Now we see but a poor reflection as in a mirror; then we
> shall see face-to-face. Now I know in part; then I shall
> know fully, even as I am fully known.

This will be the basic substance of the sermon, but the
applications are numerous.

Is there real 'Life' in the Church?

One of the greatest problems facing churches today is confusion over eschatology, and a proper understanding of these
words of Jesus will go a long way to helping restore a proper
biblical perspective. Where teaching has over-emphasised the
already-realised aspect of the life we have in Jesus, churches
have all too easily become focused on the present life and
experience of the believer, as though heaven itself were here
now. This causes Christians to lose sight of the great New
Testament emphasis on the stark reality of the struggle that
is promised to the church throughout the ages. It also tends
to play down the very real struggles with sin in the life of
believers which will not cease until that day of the final redemption of our bodies, and the final resurrection. All kinds
of problems result when expectations of the unremitting joy
and peace of the kingdom life are shattered by the harsh realities of a world still groaning in bondage to sin, and longing
for final release. Too many tender Christian lives have been
maimed by the failure of leaders to teach responsibly about
the reality of what is still 'not yet', even for the Spirit-filled
Christian. Some attention to the great 'Spirit-Life' chapter,
Romans 8, would clearly emphasise the point here, especially
8:18-24, which speaks of the present sufferings and the future
glory amid a world where not only does the believer groan,
but the whole creation is groaning, awaiting that great day
when we shall be at last raised incorruptible.

On the other hand, there is the other extreme of under-realised eschatology, where the focus is so exclusively on the 'not yet' that one is left wondering whether there is any scrap of comfort to be found for the believer in this dark world of sin. Are we left alone merely to cling on grimly while we await a Saviour from heaven, hoping desperately to last the course, even if it be by the skin of our teeth? Surely not! Often, of course, this latter emphasis is driven by reaction – or, rather, over-reaction – to the former imbalance. But it is equally wrong and equally dangerous. Where churches lose sight of the 'now' of the life that is ours in Jesus, by under-emphasising or ignoring the already-realised aspect of our salvation, and the reality of our union with Christ by the Holy Spirit, then the result is Christian lives which become dry and arid, and churches which are cold, mechanical and intellectual, empty of joy and the fragrance of the presence of Christ.

Imbalance in this direction has the effect of wearing people down with a yoke they cannot bear. Then, paradoxically, they often end up veering to the opposite extreme, in search of the 'something' that clearly is lacking in their Christian life and experience, only to land up in the unrealism of 'full gospel' experiences of those with a hopelessly over-realised eschatology. But who can blame them? Any promising spring will do in a dry and arid land. Far better to make sure we teach a full gospel in the first place, and not forget the wonderful fullness that is ours in Christ even now.

A useful cross-reference would be the opening verses of 1 Peter where, in the context of a supremely realistic view of the struggle of this life, he is nevertheless extravagant in reminding the hard-pressed believers of the wonders of their life even now: new birth into a living hope, the joyful influence already of the imperishable inheritance that is ours in Christ, the comfort in the great power of God that keeps us, and, despite trials, the rejoicing in him with joy unspeakable and full of glory (1 Pet. 1:3-8).

So, there is sermon two: the life Jesus gives, fully expounded. John 6:25-59 is simply bursting with life, both the life now and the life to come. The task of the preacher is not to seek a kind of middle path that thereby downplays either one element or the other, or both. Rather, it is to give full weight to the wonders of both the 'now' and the 'not yet'. This is the biblical perpendicular; only this can build a church that will stand.

(3) God's work and man's work
Theme three is belief, which also includes unbelief. By now we are becoming accustomed to the vivid pictures John gives of those who turn away from Jesus, and these studies in unbelief help make clearer by way of contrast exactly what constitutes saving faith. For a sermon on this theme, verses 28-29 might well set the scene:

> Then they asked him, 'What must we do to do the works
> God requires ?' Jesus answered: 'The work of God is this:
> to believe in the one he has sent.'

What we have in this chapter on this theme of belief is a classic account of both divine sovereignty demonstrated in free grace, and human responsibility demonstrated in doing what God requires, namely believing in the Son he has sent. Just as in the discussion above about the life that is in Jesus, both of these elements must be dealt with fairly and squarely.

Human responsibility: man's work is to believe
Because this section in John teaches the necessity of the divine initiative in salvation, one of the great doctrines

of John's Gospel, the preacher must not nullify human responsibility if he is to be faithful to the text. There is no hyper-Calvinism here; there is nothing in John 6 that shuts people up to fatalism, to an imposed inaction, and often to despair. Notice in verse 35 that belief is equated with an active *coming* to Jesus. According to verse 36 Jesus upbraids his hearers for not believing despite all that they have seen and heard. Verse 37 shows that the hallmarks of those the Father gives to Jesus is that they *come* to him and are not driven away as unwelcome. We are exhorted to look to the Son (40) and to listen and learn from the Father (45). We are all to eat and drink (35) and unless we do we have no life in us. There is no question here of forced feeding!

As the preacher notes these patterns of human response, he must preach just what they say, neither more nor less. We should not worry if we are then dismissed as Arminian; there have always been those for whom any preaching that calls for a response of faith instinctively elicits such a charge. If we read anything of church history (which we ought to, far more than we do) we will soon see that many of our most staunchly Calvinist forebears, such as George Whitfield and Charles Spurgeon, were often branded thus because of their zeal in evangelism. But we must not be afraid to entreat men and women to repent and believe. There are no great rewards in heaven for preachers who watch sinners heading for destruction and fail to give a word of exhortation after the pattern of Peter at Pentecost: 'Save your souls from this corrupt generation.' That great Calvinist, William Carey, never left behind his shoemaking to become the father of modern missions by listening to the voices of hyper-Calvinism in his day. Rather, he was true to his solid biblical convictions that God does indeed use 'means' for the conversion of the heathen. At the same time, of course, he would have regarded evangelistic endeavour in India as an absolutely hopeless venture without his solid assurance of divine sovereignty and salvation. John 6, then, clearly teaches that man's work is to believe; and the preacher's work includes the responsibility of calling men and women to believe.

Divine sovereignty: it is God's work alone to grant life
As we turn to the divine side in this section we find that it is crystal clear. We must not preach verse 37b without verse 37a:

> All that the Father gives me will come to me, and whoever comes to me will never be driven away.

Notice those who come to him and are not driven away are those that the Father has given to Jesus. It is those that the Father gives to the Son who alone will never perish. Verse 44 repeats the same great truth on which all Christian assurance depends:

> No one can come to me unless the Father who sent me draws him, and I will raise him up at the last day.

It is worth emphasising that the context in which these great truths about the sovereign election of God are given is that of assurance, as indeed is the case so often in the New Testament (cf. Rom. 8:28ff.). In both these verses here, notice the wonderful comfort and peace that flows from the calling of the Father: complete certainty of acceptance with God when we come to him, and sure and certain hope of the resurrection to eternal life. To that could be added complete confidence of perseverance from the day we come to him, right up until the day of resurrection: no-one can snatch us out of his hand (10:28-29). Incidentally, Don Carson has a helpful note on Peter's confident words in verse 69, and Jesus' sobering response (70), which space forbids us treating here.

So, a sermon on saving belief from this great Johannine discourse must major on both the activity of God and the activity of man. The only actual evidence that God is giving sinners to Jesus is that sinners are coming to Jesus. We could elaborate on the application of the failure to take both these elements seriously, along the lines of the discussion on life now, and life then, as would be necessary in the exposition, but since we are not writing the sermon, in this case we shall leave it for the preacher's own reflection in the study!

Before leaving this last theme in section two let us make very brief comment on verses 51 ff.

> I am the living bread that came down from heaven. If anyone eats of this bread, he will live forever. This bread is my flesh, which I will give for the life of the world.

In these words Jesus turns to speak not of the church's sacraments, but of his coming sacrifice for sinners, the benefits of which we must personally appropriate for ourselves, or perish. The whole point of his argument in these verses is that not only does Christ give the bread of life to men, he is himself that bread. And, therefore, it is in a personal relationship with him that souls are fed and satisfied. Carson, in his long and helpful treatment of the relation of John 6 to the Lord's supper, quotes Colin Brown: 'John 6 is not about the Lord's Supper, rather the Lord's Supper is about what is described in John 6.' Surely in this succinct statement is all that needs to be said. Catholic teaching on the sacrament is a tragedy, since millions believe that by partaking of the mass they are thereby eating Christ's flesh and drinking Christ's blood, and so feel assured of ultimate salvation. But as verse 63 says so pertinently the flesh counts for nothing. As for drinking Christ's blood, it may be that the astonishing episode in David's life, recorded in 2 Samuel 23:14-17 sheds some light on the unspeakable privilege of partaking in the cup of salvation in the supper of the Lord.

The Offence of the Word of the Cross

We shall only skate over this third section, verses 61-71. Much shorter than the others, it nevertheless contains the familiar elements of testimony, faith and life, though the dominant theme is clearly that of faith: the reactions of belief and unbelief that divide those who had hitherto been disciples.

As far as testimony is concerned, John's point here seems to be that it was not so much because they did not understand Jesus' words that they found them hard, but because they did grasp something of their implication, and shrank from them. This is not surprising, since it is virtually impossible not to see Jesus' words in 51 and 53 as clearly pointing to the reality of sacrifice and death, and his words about sharing in that experience (53-56) as promising costly spiritual commitment. The problem was not in understanding his challenge, but in accepting it (as the NIV makes clear in verse 61). Is not this the scandal produced by the message of the cross in every age? Indeed, the element of life that is emphasised here is that of the spiritual life which is in the very word that Jesus has spoken (63). That word, as we have seen, is the clear and unequivocal word of the cross; it is the gospel of the cross of Christ. That alone is the great fountain of life. It is in giving himself to the cross in death that makes him the bread of life for the world. Here, as throughout John's Gospel, the focus is always towards the cross as the great climax from which every blessing of the life he proclaims will flow.

But of course the cross, and the gospel of the cross, is also the great divider of men. It is the light that streams from the cross that sheds light on every man (1:9) and forces the distinction, the drawing into that light or the flight into darkness. That is the dominant emphasis in this painful conclusion to the chapter. The division could hardly be more stark, as epitomised by the contrast between verses 61 and 68b-69:

> This is a hard teaching. Who can accept it?
> Lord, to whom shall we go? You have the words of eternal life. We believe and know that you are the Holy One of God.

The word and the presence of Jesus divide. The cross of Jesus divides. And we should note here that it divides among those who were not complete strangers, but for a time, perhaps a considerable time, his followers. Why was the message so offensive (61)? Surely because the clear implications of these words are that true discipleship means a shared crucifixion, a real spiritual death, and a new creation that leaves all merely carnal concerns a thing of the past (Gal 2:20; 2 Cor 5:17). It means a captivity into obedience, bound to a Saviour with an exclusive claim upon our lives; and this is something that the natural heart of man will do anything to avoid. Throughout the whole discourse on the bread of life, the people sought to turn things back from the spiritual to the material. They were clearly attracted by the offer of life, but were held back by their earth-bound interests. And so they 'turned back and no longer followed him' (66). Having been offered the bread of life, they went away unfilled, and unblessed.

If preaching on this section, it would probably be natural to home in on the two alternatives in the form of a question: the hard and unacceptable teaching (lit. *word*) or the words of eternal life? Perhaps it could be the last of a series of sermons on this chapter, broken up similarly to the way we have done. You would have opportunity to give emphasis to that question of response to all that John has been proclaiming about Jesus, and to the fact that there are only these two alternatives. This is the real challenge to discipleship: counting the cost of the way of the cross.

7

The Key in the Rest of the Gospel

We hope that by now we have found the clearest possible indication of John's evangelistic method. We have certainly found evidence of the 'key' elements of 20:30-31 throughout the passages studied so far, and found this to be unequivocal and purposeful. Hopefully, having seen this, we shall have a better insight into these marvellous chapters, particularly with a view to teaching the gospel of Christ from them.

This little book is purposefully short. Thin books are surely the busy preacher's friend! But it is only a start, and further study must of course be done. We have only scratched the surface of the many riches that still remain to be expounded; but perhaps in so scratching we shall have excited the ambition of the preacher to dig deeper. At any rate, that has been the aim. But before we draw our study to a conclusion, we shall take the briefest of glances at the rest of John's Gospel and draw attention to the 'key' elements to see if they are anything like as pervasive as we have found them to be in the early chapters of the book.

Coming to his own

Scholars have long differed as to how the Gospel is to be divided up and analysed, and here is not the place to add further to that discussion. One wonders at times whether each new commentator feels it incumbent upon himself to find some great new illumination as to John's structure in order to justify the new work! But broadly speaking, most are agreed that the Gospel falls into two major halves, even if the exact 'turning point' is disputed. What cannot be doubted is that there is certainly a change of emphasis and tone with the beginning of chapter thirteen. The long awaited 'hour' is now imminent (13:1). A critical climax has been reached in terms of the 'many' who have believed and 'gone over' to Jesus (10:41; 11:45; 12:11,19) but also for those who are hardened in unbelief and bitter opposition, now determined to kill him (11:45; 12:10,19). Furthermore, Jesus now very clearly focuses his teaching directly on the disciples, those who had not turned back at his 'hard words' (6:60). As they had remained with him, so now he reveals to them the full extent of what his love really means for those who love him. We could say that the focus in the first half of the Gospel has been on Jesus coming to his own who, for the most part 'did not receive him' (1:11). Here, though, from 13:1 onwards, Jesus begins to expound what it means for those who did receive him, who did believe in his name, to become 'sons of God'. The focus is pre-eminently on the privileges of fellowship with the Father and the Son through the Holy Spirit.

Since virtually all of our discussion so far has been from the first portion of the Gospel, we shall not make further comment on the material up to the end of chapter 10. Suffice to say that if one continues reading the text on the lookout for our old friends testimony, belief (or unbelief) and life, the familiar pattern will quickly become apparent, and John's purpose ought to fall into place easily. Indeed, the section headings in the NIV draw attention to some of the familiar emphases quite explicitly. But we shall make a few very brief comments on the material in chapters 11-19.

Resurrection and Death:
John 11-12

It does seem that the end of chapter 10 purposely concludes a long section, bracketed by the references to ministry in Bethany trans-Jordan: first that of John (1:19-28) then that of Jesus himself (10:40-42). Incidentally, is this latter text not one crying out to be preached on?

> John did no miracle: but all things that John spoke of this man were true. And many believed on him there.

What a wonderful testimony to the greatest of the prophets! It is remarkably rare to read in the Gospels of anywhere where *many* believed in Jesus, and when we do it is notable that it is not associated with miracles. Indeed, the one place in John where it is associated with the signs, we are clearly told it is spurious faith (2:23). But here, in the last evangelistic campaign before Jesus turns his face towards Jerusalem and his approaching passion, he returns to the place where it all began, where John's dogged ministry had so faithfully proclaimed the gospel in those early days. 'And in *that* place, many believed in Jesus'! What an encouragement that ought to be to us plodding preachers who do no great miracle, to soldier on speaking the truth about the Saviour.

The turning point

Chapters 11 and 12, then, are something of a transition into the second half of the Gospel. They do provide a real turning point, since it is the giving of life to Lazarus that brings about Jesus' death; this is the final act that galvanises the opposition and sets in motion a chain of events that leads to Jesus' arrest and trial. These chapters straddle the climax of the revelatory signs that reveal Jesus for who he really is: God himself. But at the same time, they begin the exposition of the true meaning of 'the hour' and the work that Jesus came to do. The whole focus is on death and resurrection, and this becomes the preoccupation of the rest of the Gospel. What we have in the raising of Lazarus is a living enactment, a living prophecy of the victory of the Son of God over the great enemy, death itself. We are told the dead shall hear the voice of the Son of God and live (5:25), and here it is before our eyes. Here, then, is the climax of the revelation of the great theme of *life*: 'I am the resurrection and the life' (11:25). Here also is the clearest *testimony* to Jesus the giver of life from the dead: in the miracle itself, but also from his own lips (25-26) and from Martha's (27). And here too is the climactic watershed in *belief and unbelief* (45ff) as many put their faith in him, but the Jewish opposition commit themselves irreversibly to putting an end to him.

But here, notice, the order is resurrection followed by death. These two chapters bring into sharp focus the message of the Gospel as a whole. For Lazarus to live, Jesus himself must face death (note the three 'therefores' in 11:45, 53, 54 that link his victory over the grave for Lazarus with his own coming death). The paradox is that it is his greatest triumph over death that makes it clear that this victory will somehow only be accomplished through his own suffering and death. It is here in these chapters that the idea of Jesus' death as substitutionary enters with clarity for the first time. Of course it is picking up on the prophetic theme of the lamb of God (1:29,36) and the good shepherd who lays down his life for the sheep (10:11). But here is clear and unmistakable substitution of his own life, not only for Lazarus, but for the 'many' of 12:24. So, the testimony about Jesus in these chapters takes a definite turn towards testimony about his *work*, as well as testimony about his person. Jesus is seen here supremely as divine, God himself, the giver of life. Martha's great eschatological hope for resurrection from the dead is already present in his person; that is the point (11:24-26). But, the only way that this is to be realised is through the death of Jesus on the cross. Hence the testimony also to the unmistakable humanity of Jesus, and his anger and real horror in the face of death, both that of Lazarus (11:33-35) and his own as it approaches (12:27).

These chapters, then, are full of the resurrection *life* that is in Jesus. But now there is also much more on the substitutionary death that must be the grounds of that life for the many, and the great exposition of this from the lips of the Lord himself. They are full of *testimony* about Jesus, and the testimony comes from all sides: from Jesus himself, John's words about him, from the crowds, from Mary's prophetic anointing, from the Scriptures, from the lips of the High Priest – even from the voice of heaven itself. It is unmistakable testimony to both the person and work of Jesus, the Christ, the Son of God, the glory of God, the Son of Man who is lifted up to die. Moreover, we have perhaps the climax of the theme of *belief* and *unbelief*: 'the whole world' of both Jews and Gentiles are coming to him, yet the dark flight into unbelief is nevertheless never more chillingly clear; some, despite all, 'still would not believe in him.'

So all our themes are here in an unmistakable way showing John's purpose has not changed. He lays out the testimony

– now clearly including the truth about life only through death – in order to preach the way to life. The last little section of 12:44-50 gives a condensed summary, replete with all these themes, in the words of Jesus' last recorded public preaching (on which see Bruce Milne's excellent commentary in his BST volume[15]). It would make an excellent concluding sermon of a series of studies on chapters 11-12.

The Upper Room and the Passion Narrative: John 13-19

If the key is clearly evident in chapters 11 and 12, do these elements continue through the great chapters of the upper room discourses, and the passion narratives of chapters 18 and 19? By now it ought not to surprise us that indeed they do! We can make only the briefest of comments here, but of course the preacher will want to make a much closer study to be sure in his own mind that we are not forcing too much on to the text rather than reading out of it.

In a sense what we have in these chapters now is a reversal of John's usual pattern, of the sign followed by the exposition. Here, we have the discourses explaining the significance of all that was to happen, followed by the event itself in the passion narrative. Scholars argue about how many signs John means us to count in his presentation of the gospel, and whether the death and resurrection itself should be counted in as the final sign of them all. Whatever the answer to that question, what is beyond any doubt is that the death and resurrection of Jesus is the substance that every sign points to. This alone is the great denouement that has been anticipated from the very first words of the prologue. For John all testimony, all

15. *The Message of John* (Leicester: IVP, 1993).

belief, all life find their fullest meaning here. This, at last, is the full revelation of the promised glory (1:14).

Testimony then and now

First, let us turn to the theme of testimony. Consistent with what we have found to be the case in the transitional chapters 11 and 12, the nature of the testimony now focuses increasingly on the work of Jesus the Messiah, in terms of his coming death, resurrection and ascension. Again, we have testimony from many quarters, including Jesus' own testimony to his coming betrayal (13:20) and, at his trial, to the truth about his identity (18:23, 37), to pick just two examples. We have John's eyewitness testimony at the cross to the fulfilment of Scripture (19:34ff), the testimony of Pilate who could find him only innocent (19:6, 12), and the clear testimony of the titulus on the cross proclaiming his kingship in the languages of all the world (19:20) and so on, with many more bearing witness to Jesus.

But there is also a new development of the whole theme of testimony here, particularly in the farewell discourses. In addition to the multiple testimonies of the signs and wonders and the many witnesses to Jesus, there is, in Jesus' teaching on the coming Pentecostal age, a new emphasis on the testimony that will be given to Jesus by the disciples, and indeed all believers, in the future. Among the key verses here are 15:26-27.

> When the Counsellor comes, whom I will send to you from the Father, the Spirit of truth who goes out from the Father, he will testify about me. And you also must testify, for you have been with me from the beginning.

The Spirit will testify to the apostles, those who had shared a unique relationship with Jesus (Acts 1:21ff), that they too might bear unique witness to Jesus following his ascension to glory. The importance of this cannot be overstated, and indeed the careful study of this theme, and its crucial relationship to the nature of the ministry of the Holy Spirit in Chapters 14-17 is worthy of a book all of its own. Suffice to say here that the context demands that we take notice of the clear connection Jesus makes between the Holy Spirit's testimony to Jesus, the apostles' future testimony to Jesus, and the Spirit's impending work in teaching the apostles 'all things' and guiding them into 'all truth' (14:25-26; 16:13-15).

This unique ministry of the Spirit among the apostles was primarily tied to the future witness of the gospel, and was a vital factor if that gospel was going to be complete and whole, containing 'all truth'. It would not be so without the uniquely inspired interpretation of the person and work of Christ preached and recorded by these apostles. One clear implication is that the epistles (and the Gospels themselves), which encapsulate the apostolic witness, are the extension of the ministry of Jesus himself and are inspired and authoritative in exactly the same way. Their testimony to Jesus is his own testimony to himself. But a further crucial implication is that all future testimony to Jesus that can be called in any way authoritative and trustworthy must also be tied both to the testimony of the apostolic eyewitnesses and to the unique testimony of the Holy Spirit given to them. There must be a true apostolic succession if we today are to have direct access to the historical Jesus and his authoritative words, which alone are spirit and life (John 6:63). This we have in, and only in, the written word of their inspired testimony. 'These things are written' says John 'that you may believe and have life' (20:31). The clear implication is that were these things not written, we could not have life. The living, risen, ascended Christ cannot be known apart from the Christ of the Scriptures making himself known in them through the Spirit of truth.

Life now and then

The theme of life is also prominent in these later chapters of John. As discussed already in the section on chapters 11 and 12, the focus is much more clearly on life through (and only through) the death of Jesus. This is particularly clear in the famous 14:6 'I am the way, the truth and the life. No-one comes to the Father except through me.'

In the context we must be clear that the 'but through me' refers to his approaching death. He is going to prepare a place for them in his Father's house for eternity, not after but through his death. Only if this is accomplished will he return to receive them to be with him for eternity (14:3); hence the priority of the message of the risen Jesus to the disciples: 'I *am* returning to my Father and your Father' (20:17) – in other words, your future hope is secure.

But there is also much emphasis on the life that is ours now, as well as the life to come. Chapter 17, the great prayer of Jesus, is full of eternal life experienced already as the knowledge of the Father made possible through Jesus (17:3). And just as the theme of testimony is developed to include the testimony of the apostles and all future believers to Jesus, so too the theme of life is developed here to include the fruit that is the result of that life at work in those who are his own, who have received him. The fruit of this life is evident in chapter 15 in particular, with its famous teaching on Jesus as the true vine. The primary fruit of the life to come breaking into the here and now in Christian faith is that of loving relationship and intimacy with the Father and the Son: abiding in that love as friends of Jesus (15:5, 9-10, 14-15; cf. 14:23), and enjoying the intimacy of prayer, another defining characteristic of the life of God at work in the soul of man (cf. Acts 9:11). It is from this primary fruit of living relationship that all other fruit-bearing flourishes and multiplies as, notice, fruitful branches are pruned and trimmed through ongoing costly obedience to the word of truth (15:3-4, 10). Life comes through death in the believer's experience, just as life came through death for the Son of God.

Belief, love and obedience

Belief is also prominent in these chapters, and as before it is very closely tied to the themes of testimony and life. Again, the focus now is much more strongly on the cross, and the death of Jesus. Jesus' testimony in advance about his betrayal and his death is explicitly tied to faith: 'I have told you now before it happens so that when it does happen you will believe' (13:19; 14:29). Looking at the passion narrative, we find that John draws attention not only to John's testimony about the water and the blood 'so that you may believe' (19:35) but also to the little cameo appearance of Nicodemus which is so full of significance. Here is 'the man who had earlier visited Jesus at night' (19:39), who had crept towards the light by voicing a measure of support for Jesus before the Pharisees (7:50), but who now comes right out into the light at the foot of the cross.

Belief is also focused on hearing and accepting the words of Jesus, which are not simply his own but the words of the Father himself (14:10). And such belief in the Son's exclusive relationship with the Father is tied to the love (and life) that the Father himself gives to those who so believe (16:27).

But here too there is an added dimension to the theme of belief for those who have come into the light and accepted the testimony about Jesus. For not only will they believe, and know the joy of the high priestly prayers of Jesus on their behalf (17:8), through their testimony others also will believe. Just as Jesus gave them the word the Father had given him, so the disciples would give to others their word (informed by the Spirit) that they too might believe and come into the same knowledge of the Father and Son (17:20). Belief, too, is found to be intimately related to the apostolic testimony, and to the word of the New Testament Scriptures. It is also intimately related to love for Jesus. To trust in him is to love him (14:1, 15); and the proof of love is obedience to his word (14:15, 21-23).

> To know him is to love him, and to love him is to obey his commands. If we remembered this, we would be delivered from a great deal of confusion in spiritual life.
>
> James Philip

The Fruit Of Testimony, Faith And Life In Jesus

For those who have believed, then, to whom he has given the right to become children of God, who have been born of God, testimony, belief and life take on a new dimension. They become not only external, but internal. To truly believe in Jesus is not merely to accept the claims about his person; it is to know him in his death and resurrection, to find life through death. To know that life is to share in its example, in the ongoing experience of dying to live, of serving as he served. This is what it means to abide in him, to abide in his love and to bear fruit in obedience to him. This is what it means to have eternal life now. And this life, this 'abiding in him' that goes on bearing fruit for eternity is nurtured and sustained as his word – the apostolic gospel – abides in us.

So, we find that our three old friends, the elements of John's 'key' have not deserted us as we have scouted through the remaining pages of John's Gospel. Rather, they have remained our steady companions to the end, and shown themselves to be larger than life, particularly in these great central chapters of the upper room discourses. Much more could be said, and would need to be said; we have raised many more questions and issues than we have adequately dealt with. But there is room here only for a brief conclusion, and to that we turn.

8

Passing On John's Preaching

Having considered very briefly the message of John's Gospel as a whole, and focused in some detail on just a few of the sections of this great fourth Gospel, we have been able to show something of John's self-proclaimed evangelistic purpose in action. The hope is that this may give the Bible teacher, and especially the preacher planning a series on some or all of John's Gospel, a way in to the text. The goal is modest, but we hope practical; the end in sight is not the exegetical essay for the professor, but the weekly nourishment of the people of God. Hence we have always tried to keep in view the preacher, and perhaps most important of all, the listener.

Learning to listen
We have given no more than a start, a taster of the many wonders that lie within the pages of John's book, and await patient and prayerful excavation in the preacher's study. Yet

our conviction is that John does not merely present us in his writing with raw materials for us to work into a message for preaching. Rather, he himself has already worked the events to which he is a witness into proclamation – preaching – of his own, according to his pattern of testimony (or evidence), faith and life declared in John 20:30-31. In so doing he plays his own part in fulfilling the promise of Jesus in John 16:12-15, namely that the apostles themselves would be the unique vehicles of the Spirit's work of bringing the full and final revelation of 'all truth' to the church. Their interpretation, in their uniquely inspired writing in the Gospels and Epistles, are for us the authoritative interpretation of the words and work of Christ. This, and this alone, is 'the faith which was once for all delivered to the saints' (Jude 3). The Gospel before us, like the Epistles and indeed the whole Scripture, is Christ speaking to his church. The Bible *is* God preaching!

Learning to speak

So, we have sought to listen to John preaching, telling us how he interprets the truth about Jesus in his Gospel. If we have heard him properly, then we should be reliable heralds of his message. What a relief it is to find that ours is not the task of interpreting the stories about Jesus! John, under the unique influence of the infallible Spirit of God, has done so already. Our task as pastor-teachers and servants of the word today is, quite simply, to listen to his fully inspired preaching on its own terms, and to pass it on faithfully to others in our own preaching (2 Tim 2:2). We must do so, of course, with all seriousness and reverence. We are not infallible and uniquely inspired. We cannot master the word of God. But it must master us. We must work hard with all the energy God gives us to present ourselves as worthy workmen who do not need to be ashamed, who 'rightly divide the word of truth' (2 Tim 2:15). We use all the helps we can find, by way of commentaries and other study aids. Above all we come to the Scriptures in total dependence upon the Spirit of God: not to 'inspire' the word afresh (it *is* the once-for-all inspired word) but to breathe it out to us, to illumine our dark minds and hearts to grasp it and submit to it, and to strengthen and enable our weak efforts to proclaim it. We should not miss the significance that John intends by recording Jesus' great prayer (Ch. 17) as inseparable from his foregoing sublime exposition of the meaning of his coming death and resurrection (Ch. 13-16). Just as we must not separate the word and the Spirit of God, in either theology or practice, so we cannot separate prayer and the preaching of the word (cf. Acts 6:4). Prayer-less preaching is an oxymoron.

Preaching John's Gospel Today

> These are written that you may believe that Jesus is the Christ, the Son of God, and that by believing you may have life in his name.
>
> John 20:31

We end where we began, with John's own self-proclaimed purpose. His method is still vital today. It should offer us great help in our own preaching from all the Scriptures, but especially from his own Gospel. But please note, we are certainly *not* suggesting that anyone should preach a series through the whole Gospel, each sermon with three headings: evidence, faith, life. That would be to risk terminal boredom in both preacher and people! Much of what we have drawn out is only the scaffolding; it helps in the work of design and building but ultimately must be taken down and remain in the study rather than intruding into the final message. Yet, having worked to discern John's priorities for his own presentation of the message, surely we shall have a much better chance of keeping in step with his aims as we pass that message on to our hearers today. So, let us summarise very briefly the key conclusions.

Preach Life

It is surely right to emphasise the reality of the life that there is in Jesus. With young people especially we want to point to the Lord Jesus in terms of John 10:10. 'I have come that they may have life, and have it to the full.' Jesus is no killjoy! There may, however, still be a reluctance to give the full message of life – not only life now, but resurrection on the last day. Experience with young people is that a reluctance to include this future life in our message is quite mistaken. They need to know, and often long to know, of Christ's great victory over death, and of the hope of glory. After all, young people and teenagers these days are no strangers to stresses and strains, to griefs and sorrows. They need the 'strength for today, and bright hope for tomorrow' that the full gospel gives as much as anybody else does. The answer is to preach both now and then, life in the present and life to come. Remember the living experience Jesus offered the Samaritan woman here and now? That is the best possible preventative to seeking for satisfaction in drugs, sexual permissiveness and hedonism generally. So let us preach the true life of the new age both in its present form and experience and in its future promise and manifestations.

Preach the evidence

To find life we must find God, and faith in God. How does this come to pass? The apocryphal story of the curate who asked his bishop what to preach about is familiar enough.

The answer came: 'preach about God and about twenty minutes'! But how does John preach about God? As we have seen, he preaches about Jesus and his words and his works in their historical context. In student missions today missioners frequently take one of the four Gospels as the basis for the addresses. Surely there can be no better way of listening to and learning from the Father than listening to and learning from the Son. Of course this must never mean collapsing the historical record into the present. Rather, it means listening to the Gospel writer's own proclamation of the truth of the gospel, absorbing his message in its context then, and proclaiming his message again to the people today, so that it can be seen clearly to originate in the Word of God open before us. We preach the evidence, the testimony in Scripture to Jesus Christ, the one and only, who alone has made known the Father.

Preach for a verdict

Finally, the evangelistic method of John faces the hearer with the immediate consequences of faith and rejection, the only alternatives.

> Whoever believes in him is not condemned but whoever does not stands condemned already ... Whoever believes in the Son has eternal life but whoever rejects the Son will not see life for God's wrath remains on him.
>
> John 3:18, 36

The word of the gospel divides. It calls forth a crisis in the hearts of men and women, the crisis of belief and unbelief. We must proclaim the message with this firmly in mind, knowing that it is the message itself that is the scandal, and knowing that faithful proclamation cannot avoid it. Nor should we try to. Nevertheless, our hearts must surely be filled with the grace and compassion of our Lord himself, who though hated by the world came to save even the religious ignorants, nobodies and degenerates of this world, and offered them the water of life. We preach not for condemnation, but for faith. Our purpose must be that of John himself, for all that he wrote was in order that his readers might believe that Jesus is the Christ, the Son of God, and that by coming to believe in him they might have life in his name.

9
Further Resources
for Preaching on John

The aim of this book has been to act as a starter for the expositor; to whet the appetite and encourage the preacher to take the plunge and begin working towards a serious attempt to teach through this wonderful Gospel. Obviously the resources available, particularly commentaries, are legion, and one could feel spoiled for choice and hardly know where to start. In this section we draw attention to just a few places that the expositor might look to for further help. It should not be regarded as a list of 'sound' or 'hallmarked' sources! As we have commented already, wide reading is to be encouraged. But neither time nor money is unlimited, and we must be realistic.

Commentaries and Expositions on John's Gospel
It is generally wise to have one, or perhaps two, trusted conservative commentaries on the text which can be relied upon to keep you on the straight and narrow. But on the

other hand, one should never have too high an expectation of any commentary as far as helping the actual sermon is concerned. The clearest and soundest can be the driest and dullest! We would encourage reading anything you find on the bookshelf or can pick up cheaply, because often it may be just a single sentence from the most unlikely source that sparks the most fruitful thinking for the preacher. Here we give mention to some of the books found most useful and some of those alluded to in this present study.

Don Carson's Pillar Commentary, *The Gospel According to John* (IVP, 1991) is one of the most useful 'solid' commentaries on the text. It deals with the original text, but quoted Greek is transliterated and therefore very accessible. It is very useful for extended discussion of controversial topics, though not always inspirational as far as helping the preacher get to his sermon; but probably a 'must have'. Another useful and fairly conservative exegetical commentary with some penetrating insights is **CK Barrett**, *The Gospel According to St. John* (SPCK, 1978). We have also used and quoted from **Ridderbos** *The Gospel Of John: A Theological Commentary* (Eerdmans, 1997) and from **Leon Morris** in the NICNT series, which is also excellent and has some real gems in the footnotes. As always, **Calvin** is brilliant at getting to the heart of the significance and the theological implications of the text with the expositon firmly in mind. The modern translation (Eds DW & TF Torrance) is the most accessible, but you can pick up the Victorian translation quite cheaply. (You can now also get Calvin's entire works on CD ROM from Ages Software, and many of his writings are accessible free on the internet.)

A totally different kind of work is **Mark Stibbe's** Readings commentary *John* (JSOT, 1993). This is quite a short book, taking a narrative critical approach to the text, and is a very stimulating read. We would have definite differences of view on many matters, so would not urge uncritical reading, but it is brilliantly sensitive to John's wonderful dramatic touch, and actually very helpful indeed to the preacher. Read it alongside Carson.

For a book that is more expositional in nature, it is hard to beat **Bruce Milne's** superb BST *The Message of John* (IVP, 1993), so obviously written by a preacher for fellow Bible teachers. The challenge is in not just reproducing his expositions! It is also well worth consulting some of the older more expositional commentaries, which at times can seem flowery in language to us, but very often get to the heart of the matter for the preacher better than anything newer. The notes sections in **J C Ryle's Expository Thoughts on John** are a mine of helpful (and often very quotable) pithy sayings and quotes from older divines, and the works by **William Temple, G Campbell-Morgan** and **Alexander Maclaren** are well worth picking up if you see them second hand. Other commentaries we have mentioned include **Plummer** and **Westcott**, which despite provoking many differences of opinion, have many useful insights and often a very good turn of phrase.

All of these have pros and cons; there is no such thing as a perfect commentary. There are numerous others, many of them with very useful contributions to make, and it is always worth a glance at anything you can get your hands on. Just don't expect any one to strike gold with consistency. If we had to plump for a fistful, it would be Calvin, Carson, Stibbe, Milne and Ryle.

PT Media

RESOURCES FOR PREACHERS AND BIBLE TEACHERS

PT Media, a ministry of The Proclamation Trust, provides a range of multimedia resources for preachers and Bible teachers.

Books
The *Teach the Bible* commentary series, published jointly with *Christian Focus Publications*, is specifically geared to the purpose of God's Word – its proclamation as living truth. Books in this series offer practical help for preachers or teachers tackling a Bible book or doctrinal theme. Current titles are: *Teaching Matthew, Teaching John, Teaching Acts, Teaching 1 Peter, Teaching Amos* and *Teaching the Christian Hope*. Forthcoming titles include: *Teaching Mark, Teaching Daniel, Teaching Isaiah, Teaching Romans, Teaching Nehemiah, Teaching 1, 2, 3 John, Teaching Ephesians, Teaching 1&2 Samuel*.

DVDs

Preaching & Teaching the Old Testament:
　　　Narrative, Prophecy, Poetry, Wisdom
Preaching & Teaching the New Testament:
　　　Gospels, Epistles, Acts & Revelation

These interactive DVD-based training resources (including down-loadable workbooks in pdf format) are based on the core 'Principles of Exposition' element from the Cornhill Training Course. Taught by David Jackman, founder-director of Cornhill, and now President of The Proclamation Trust, the material is designed for individual study, group study or use as part of a training course.

Dick Lucas' *Instructions On Biblical Preaching* ('The Un-ashamed Workman') is also available on DVD.

Audio

PT Media Audio Resources offer an excellent range of material for the preacher or Bible teacher, covering over twenty years of conferences. The *Sermons On...* series (expositions) and the *Instruction On...* series (how to teach a Bible book or doctrinal theme) are available as mp3 CDs and downloads.

For further information on these and other PT Media products, visit our website at **www.proctrust.org.uk** or email **media@proctrust.org.uk**

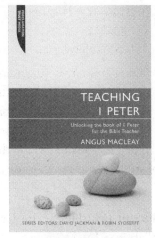

ISBN 978-1-84550-347-5

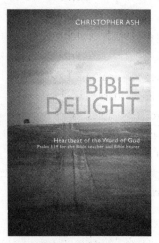

ISBN 978-1-84550-360-4

ISBN 978-1-84550-255-3

ISBN 978-1-84550-142-6

PROCLAMATION
TRUST MEDIA

TEACHING
1 PETER

Unlocking the book of 1 Peter
for the Bible Teacher

ANGUS MACLEAY

SERIES EDITORS: DAVID JACKMAN & ROBIN SYDSERFF

Teaching 1 Peter

Unlocking the book of 1 Peter for the Bible Teacher

Angus Macleay

The books are purposefully practical. Section One contains basic 'navigation' material to get you into the text of 1 Peter. Section Two works systematically through a suggested preaching or Bible study series. Preaching outlines and Bible study questions are included for each passage,

The message of 1 Peter is vital for Christians living in any generation, not least our own, showing us how we should live as God's people in a godless world.

'This volume is full of practical help for teachers and preachers, and the careful exposition of the text draws out powerfully its relevance for the 21st Century Western Church. This must be added to your library.'

Peter Maiden,
International Director of Operation Mobilization, Chairman of Keswick Ministries.

'...In whatever way we use this commentary, we will find it profitable for teaching, instruction, correction and encouragement.'

Michael Nazir-Ali,
Bishop of Rochester.

'I warmly commend this excellent resource for teachers of 1 Peter. Angus Macleay perceptively draws out the themes and shapes of the letter, provides shrewd insight into the details of the text and also offers much helpful advice about how to apply and present its material.'

Vaughan Roberts,
Rector of St Ebbe's Church, Oxford.

Angus Macleay is the minister of St. Nicholas, a large Anglican Church in Sevenoaks, Kent. He is also a member of the Church of England General Synod.

ISBN 978-1-84550-347-5

Christian Focus Publications
publishes books for all ages
Our mission statement –

STAYING FAITHFUL
In dependence upon God we seek to help make His infallible Word, the Bible, relevant. Our aim is to ensure that the Lord Jesus Christ is presented as the only hope to obtain forgiveness of sin, live a useful life and look forward to heaven with Him.

REACHING OUT
Christ's last command requires us to reach out to our world with His gospel. We seek to help fulfil that by publishing books that point people towards Jesus and help them develop a Christ-like maturity. We aim to equip all levels of readers for life, work, ministry and mission.

Books in our adult range are published in three imprints.

Christian Focus contains popular works including biographies, commentaries, basic doctrine and Christian living. Our children's books are also published in this im-print.

Mentor focuses on books written at a level suitable for Bible College and seminary students, pastors, and other serious readers. The imprint includes commentaries, doctrinal studies, examination of current issues and church history.

Christian Heritage contains classic writings from the past.

Christian Focus Publications Ltd
Geanies House, Fearn, Ross-shire,
IV20 1TW, Scotland, United Kingdom
info@christianfocus.com
www.christianfocus.com